Errata

Page 18. Footnote to Graph II-2.

* In 1944 the item was reworded slightly to read: "Do you think there should or should not be a law passed that requires every worker in a plant to belong to a union if the majority votes to have a union?"

Page 20. Footnote to Graph II-3.

* In 1965 and in 1966, arbitration proceedings would be instituted after a strike had gone on for *seven* days.

Page 40. Footnote to Graph II-4.

* In 1944, 1945, and 1946, the item read: "Do you regard the amount of tax you had to pay on your income as fair?"

Page 57. Footnotes to Graph III-1.

* Negroes were polled separately: 92 percent answered "yes."
** The item appeared in two polls in the same year: in the first, 77 percent answered "yes"; in the second, 78 percent answered in the affirmative.

Page 59. Footnote to Graph III-2.

* The school integration crisis in Little Rock, Arkansas, was at its peak during this period.

Page 60. Footnote to Graph III-3.

* The year 1969 is an exception to other years shown, wherein only parents with school-age children were sampled; in 1969 a national sample was taken that did not specify that respondents have school-age children.

Page 63. Footnote to Graph III-5.

* In 1965 and 1966, the item read: "Would you object to having a Negro with just as much income and education as you as a next-door neighbor?"

Page 68. Footnotes to Graph III-6.

* In 1961, the item read: "Do you think 'sit-ins' at lunch counters, freedom buses, and other demonstrations by Negroes will hurt or help the Negroes' chances of being integrated in the South?"
** In 1967, the item read: "Do Negroes have more to gain or more to lose by resorting to violence in the civil rights movement?"

Page 101. Footnote to Graph IV-3.

* From Bruno Bettelheim and Morris Janowitz, *Social Change and Prejudice,* Glencoe, Ill., The Free Press, 1964, p. 6.

Page 117. Footnotes to Graph V-4.

* In 1969, the item read: "Do you feel that *students* have the right to make their protests or not?"
** In 1970, the item read: "As long as there appears to be no clear danger of violence, do you think any groups, no matter how extreme, should be allowed to organize protests against the government?"

Page 155. Footnotes to Graph VI-5.

* Eisenhower and Stalin would be the participants in such a meeting.
** Eisenhower and Khrushchev would be the participants at this meeting.
*** Kennedy and Khrushchev would be the participants at this meeting.

PUBLIC OPINION
IN AMERICA

PUBLIC OPINION
IN AMERICA:
1936-1970

RITA JAMES SIMON
University of Illinois at Urbana-Champaign

A MARKHAM BOOK from
Rand McNally College Publishing Company/Chicago

Current printing (last digit)
15 14 13 12 11 10 9 8 7 6 5 4 3 2 1

For David, Judith, Daniel, and Julian

CONTENTS

LIST OF TABLES

LIST OF GRAPHS

PREFACE

The job of systematically surveying public opinion on a national scale and at regular intervals began in the United States in the second half of the 1930's. Today there are more than a dozen major American polling agencies, with large staffs and complicated techniques, that report public opinion on issues affecting all aspects of contemporary life. Elections, civil rights, population growth, antiwar demonstrations, and pollution are some of the issues reported in national surveys since 1960. During the 1930's, when the practice first began, economic matters and social welfare were the topics about which the public was most often queried.

This volume brings together national survey data on important domestic and international issues from the first surveys of the 1930's through World War II, the postwar era, the "quiet" 1950's, and the turbulent 1960's. Space limitations prohibit reporting all issues and including all surveys. Still, most of the important and continuing problems that involve domestic and foreign policy are touched on in this volume. Many of the problems that are discussed briefly in each of the chapters have been treated at length in special volumes dedicated to a history of the American labor movement, an analysis of the cold war, an investigation of the public's response to McCarthyism, an examination of population growth, and so on. The particular virtue of this book is that it provides an overview of public opinion on many issues over the full time span for which national survey data are available.

Acknowledgment is gratefully extended to the American Institute of Public Opinion (The Gallup Poll), The Roper Center, and *Public Opinion Quarterly* for permission to cite various poll data throughout the book.

I also wish to express my appreciation to Linda Mahan and Laura Monypenny for help in collecting the data, to Charles Bonjean for a thorough and critical reading of earlier drafts, and to Vivian Alsip of Urbana and Sylvia Farhi of Jerusalem for typing the manuscript.

SERIES INTRODUCTION

The present volume is one of several in a series on Process and Change in American Society that have been published under our editorship. Each of these books is intended to chart patterns of social change in one or more American institutions and/or in the processes that link these institutions.

As editors, we have encouraged the authors to utilize systematic and quantitative materials wherever these are available. We have also encouraged them to use alternative sources to fill in any appreciable gaps that are left by the quantitative record. Perhaps most important, we have encouraged the authors to present their materials in a provocative way, tying together the pieces of statistical and documentary evidence with a theoretical viewpoint, a central perspective, or a critical perspective informed by articulated ideological principles. Thus, the volumes in this series have aspired to be more than summaries of what is known about social trends and processes of change in the areas on which they focus; they have generally been intended to be essays drawing out theoretical and/or policy implications of major substantive conclusions about these areas.

Facts do not speak for themselves, and the volumes in this series have not been seen as written commentaries on statistical abstracts and historical almanacs. Their authors have attempted to organize what is known into a coherent overview from which, hopefully, the reader might see both the interrelations among what is known and the probable character of the missing pieces.

Needless to say, when much of the digging in our past and present is complete, such efforts at organizing known trends as those made in the volumes of this series will be found to have been less than fully successful. It has been hoped, however, that the accounts of change given in these books, even where the evidence is piecemeal, will have provided guideposts to directions where further excavation is likely to be quite productive.

In the present volume, Rita James Simon goes beyond the effort to piece together uneven evidence on one or a limited number of social institutions to seek to summarize a broad array of systematic data across America dealing with major social trends over 34 years. She does so by developing times series data made available by the results of scientific polling procedures that flowered across this period. This is not to indicate that all of the information has a high degree of quality or that she limits herself to those aspects of social trends on which she has a broad array of measures across time; indeed, she imaginatively seeks to combine both those sets of data which are comprehensive with those more limited ones on which reasoned qualification and even speculation must be developed.

A principal virtue of this book is that it provides the reader with a knowledge of the many areas of American public issue and opinion with which the pollsters have become concerned on a relatively continual basis. To whatever extent polling has developed principally to serve immediate journalistic and political interests, its results have frequently come to serve a variety of serious and systematic social scientific interests, ranging from the study of public attitudes toward liberal legislation, prejudice, civil liberties, and foreign policy issues. Although trends in public opinion on certain specific issues are more comprehensively studied elsewhere, this volume presents an impressive articulation of changes across the great range of issues. In addition, the author provides a sensitive account of how certain changes in opinion appear to presage political action while other changes seem to follow it.

June, 1974   Robert W. Hodge
                    University of California at Los Angeles

                                                David P. Street
                                        University of Michigan

I
INTRODUCTION

This book describes public opinion in the United States from the mid-1930's to 1970, on a variety of important and controversial questions involving domestic and foreign policy by examining the responses given on national surveys. Topics on which opinion data are reported can be divided broadly into two areas: those involving domestic issues such as social welfare, civil rights, trade unions, family planning, taxation, and civil liberties; and those probing reactions to American foreign policy. The time span for the analysis is determined by the period for which the national surveys are available.

A BRIEF OVERVIEW

The major purpose of this review is to provide a profile of American opinion over a period of time in which the society has experienced important changes. In the first period covered by this review, the United States was in the midst of the worst economic depression of its history. No problem was more urgent in the minds of the American public than that of getting the economy moving again. Other domestic social and political issues were either put aside or tied to the necessity of revitalizing the economic system. Government officials, intellectuals, aspiring politicians, radicals, academicians, and cadres of people with special skills were working on agricultural production, food distribution, the job market, foreign trade, benefits for the aged and the sick, and other socio-economic problems.

The problems on the minds of the American people in the 1930's were different from the problems most often talked about in the decade of the affluent 1960's and early 1970's. Today, domestic problems seem to arise as much from distribution and affluence as from scarcity. The phrase "fat society" is used often both to denigrate and to simply describe American society. The intellectuals tell us that "impersonality," "indifference," "bureaucracy," "technology," and just plain "bigness' are hurting the American soul, "the quality of life." The targets of attack today are as likely to be the universities and the trade unions as big business or corporations were in the 1930's. Organized labor in the 1930's, especially in the industrial unions, had allies in the youth and students of the country. Today, largely because organized labor supports the government's position on Vietnam, but also because of the relative affluence and security-consciousness of American workers, students and workers no longer share the same picket lines. Thirty-five years ago, the labor unions were young and growing, and they used militant rhetoric to criticize the establishment, of which they were clearly not a part. The strikes that occurred in Seattle, Minneapolis, Detroit, Akron, and Toledo were as militant and destructive as any this country had ever witnessed.

Federal programs that now need expanding or overhauling— such as social security, minimum wages, children's and women's working conditions, federal aid to education, medical care for the aged and the indigent, and other welfare services—were still on the drawing boards or "on trial."

The dissidents in the 1930's were often leftists and rightists who had ties to older, European-based movements. For most of the left, "Mecca" was the Soviet Union, the country that had succeeded in doing what the labor and radical movements of the more industrialized societies of Western Europe, especially Germany, had been unable to achieve. The most successful of the American leftist movements in the 1930's was the American Communist Party. On the right, the death of Huey Long, Senator from Louisiana and spokesman for small farmers and small businessmen in rural areas and small towns all over the country, left a vacuum in the home-grown variety of right-wing movements—a vacuum that was filled toward the end of the decade by Father Coughlin, Gerald L. K. Smith, and Francis Townsend. Father Coughlin's Sunday evening radio broadcasts in the late 1930's competed with President Roosevelt's "fireside chats" for the highest "Nielsen" ratings. Of less national importance, but of significant regional impact, were such groups as the Silver Shirts and the Ku Klux Klan. Along with the indigenous forms of right-wingism, there was also the German-American Bund, led by Fritz Kuhn and Joseph Kamp, that looked to Berlin for support and guidance in much the same way that the Communist Party relied on Moscow.

The threatening sounds of war in Europe were, at first, muted by domestic anxieties. The public's collective memory of America's failure at the peace table following World War I, which culminated in the Senate's vote against ratification of the League of Nations and the seeming ingratitude of the European nations for the aid given them by the United States, reinforced the traditionally isolationist tendencies of most Americans. When the noise—first from across the Atlantic and then from the Pacific—became too loud to ignore, Americans grudgingly supported the sending of aid to Britain, France, and China and started preparing for the possibility that the United States might once again "be drawn into a European war."

As the 1930's wore on, there was a sense of growing antipathy toward Nazi Germany, but the more intense concern was that whatever trouble might lie ahead for Europe or Asia would not spill over to the United States. This time France and England should not be encouraged to rely on the military and economic resources of the United States. If they were going to take on Hitler and Mussolini, they should do so with their own resources. The traditional friendship that the United States and France had enjoyed for a century and a half had soured, largely as a result of the public humiliation President Wilson had received at the hands of Clemenceau, France's senior statesman, during the peace conferences following World War I and of France's failure to repay a significant portion of the debt owed the United States. England, historically, had not experienced the friendship which France had had with the United States, and her insistence at the peace conferences on expanding her overseas empire at the cost of the defeated nations did not enhance America's estimation of her.

Thus, when our story begins, in the latter part of the 1930's, we find a nation confronting its most serious internal crisis since the Civil War and a people disillusioned by their efforts at international cooperation and indifferent to the calls for help from other nations. Domestically, the Democratic Party had promised a New Deal to the electorate and had just begun to introduce a series of major legislative innovations. Labor, youth, women, the aged, and the infirm were to be the chief beneficiaries. The image of the federal government was undergoing rapid change. The public was being educated to expect and demand services from the government that previously had not been considered appropriate. The rallying cry was "Let's get the economy moving"; after that, related problems in civil rights, education, and so on would begin to work themselves out.

But the United States could not evade the web of foreign involvement, and after December 7, 1941, debates about rightness or wrongness, preparedness or lack of preparedness became moot. For the American public, much of the 1940's was taken up with the war and with how well the United States and her allies were conducting themselves against the Axis powers. A lot of time was also devoted to debating how the United States and the Soviet Union would get along with each other after the war. About halfway through the war, the leaders of the Big Four (Roosevelt, Churchill, Stalin, and Chiang Kai-shek) decided on a policy of "unconditional surrender" vis-à-vis the enemy; the policy met with widespread approval from the American public. There was also much support for plans that were announced toward the end of the war to treat the enemy nations, especially Germany and Japan, with greater harshness than had been meted out to the losers of World War I. That Americans continued to support such a policy after the fighting ended was manifested by their approval of the war criminals' trials at Nuremberg and Tokyo, their endorsement of the military occupation of Germany and Japan, and their lack of guilt at the dropping of atomic bombs on the Japanese cities of Hiroshima and Nagasaki.

The latter part of the 1940's saw the beginning of the cold war, that in retrospect appears to have been formally recognized with Winston Churchill's Iron Curtain speech in Fulton, Missouri, in 1946. The period was also marked by debates about how much military and economic foreign aid ought to be given to which countries and about how the United States ought to conduct itself in the United Nations. Internally, the phenomenon known today as "McCarthyism" (after the junior Senator from Wisconsin, Joseph R. McCarthy) began to attract considerable attention. There was much debate about whether McCarthy was right or wrong, sincere or opportunistic, and whether his activities were helpful or harmful to the country. Other politicians, among the more notable of whom was a Representative from California, Richard M. Nixon, entered the fray; and today, the latter part of the 1940's and the early 1950's are remembered for the fervor with which communists and other subversives were sought in many spheres of American life. Legislation was passed requiring members of the Communist Party to register with the Justice Department, and trade-union leaders and college professors had to swear loyalty to the United States or face losing their jobs. The war in Korea, which began in the summer of 1950, added fuel to feelings that were already near the brink of explosion about the dangers to American security from the reds and pinks who needed to be cleared out of the State Department, the universities, the labor unions, the movie industry, and wherever else they may have taken refuge.

By the middle 1950's, most of the zeal for hunting subversives was gone. The Korean War ended in 1953, and at about the same time, Senator McCarthy challenged an opponent that proved his undoing: the United States Army. The rest of the decade is remembered for its relative stability and quiescence.

In retrospect, the "quiet" 1950's may have been the period during which the seeds were planted for the new ideas about social policy, political criticism, and styles of personal behavior and group living that burst forth seemingly fully developed in the early 1960's. The new "tone" to American society began with the election of John F. Kennedy to the Presidency and the shift of influence in Washington from Midwestern business leaders to Ivy League professors. The civil-rights movement was the focus of much of the social experimentation and criticism which then spread to other groups that directed their attacks not only at the hypocrisy inherent in white America's attitudes toward blacks, but also at policies on other social issues: welfare and education, to name the most important.

The two Kennedy assassinations, plus the assassination of Martin Luther King, Jr., and the more extensive military commitment in Vietnam, set the stage for divisiveness and bitterness between generations and between racial groups, comparable only to the class bitterness of the 1930's or the regional bitterness of the Civil War era. Students, especially those with liberal, middle-class, educated parents, turned against the symbols that their parents had taught them to revere (the labor unions, the reform wing of the Democratic Party, the moderate prointegration elements within the civil-rights movement) and with which their parents had so proudly identified. The black youth (and some over 30 as well) turned militant. "Black is beautiful," "Black wants to make it on its own," "Black is through following Whitey (even if Whitey is more educated and liberal)" became themes that characterized much of the 1960's. It was a period for the worst urban race riots in the country's history and the most severe acts of civil disorder.

At the time of writing, the war in Vietnam is still with us. Campus unrest has subsided, as has much of the urban and racial violence, but tension and concern about how these issues will be met in the future remain high. As one looks into the 1970's, one cannot help but wonder whether the conflict and violence of the 1960's will be repeated, and perhaps exacerbated, or whether they will subside. If more violence lies ahead, what changes is it likely to impose on the structure and social organization of the society? If the decade is more tranquil, what has the violence of the 1960's cost or benefited the society in terms of social integration and a sense of national purpose.

But all of this discussion is prologue. The subsequent chapters report public opinion from the 1930's through the 1960's about each of the substantive areas mentioned briefly above. The concluding chapter divides the time periods into shorter and more homogeneous units and provides a cross-sectional view of public opinion about foreign affairs and domestic issues during each period.

PUBLIC OPINION: DEFINITION AND FUNCTION

Before we turn to the first of these problems, a few comments about the nature of public opinion will be made: what public opinion is and what use can be made of its study by social scientists.

James Bryce's definition of public opinion—"the aggregate of views men hold regarding matters that affect or interest the community" (Bryce, 1962, p. 50)—is a good working definition and one that is consistent with the manner in which the poll data are used in this volume. To be more exact, in this study, public opinion is "the aggregate of views people hold regarding matters that [*the pollsters decide*] affect or interest the community." We assume that there is a good deal of overlap between these two conditions. By operationalizing our use of the national surveys and combining it with Bryce's definition, the following interpretation of public opinion emerges: the verbal responses that a representative sample of adults in the United States have made to various questions about national policy put to them by experts who tell us that these are the important issues of the day.

Interpreting public opinion in this manner raises several questions about the worthwhileness of this kind of endeavor. The first problem concerns the reliability of the public's responses. How likely is it that if the same respondent is approached a day, a week, or a month later, he will express the same opinion that he held on the first occasion, assuming of course that no external event has occurred that would make a different opinion a reasonable response. The social context in which a poll is taken is usually the doorstep or, if the pollster is lucky and the respondent polite, the respondent's living room. After the pollster has asked his questions and the subject has answered them, the pollster records the answers and leaves. Do the responses recorded at time x have any implications for how the respondent will answer those same questions at time y?

In some studies, we can measure reliability over time with a good deal of precision. Panels, for example, are set up to do exactly that. A group of people is selected to participate in a panel study, which means that on two, three, six, or more occasions the interviewer will return to the same participants and ask them what their opinions are about the initial topic. Panel studies, therefore, are set up to answer precisely how reliable a respondent's answer at time x is likely to be. Unfortunately, national polls for the kinds of issues examined in this volume have not been set up as panels. Nevertheless, we have tried to approximate panel data, whenever possible, by using questions that have been asked on more than one occasion.

On some topics, such as attitudes toward Negroes, Jews, trade unions, and taxes, almost all of the questions reported have been repeated on at least four different occasions. There are many instances in which we can trace responses to the same item over the entire span of this inquiry, namely, the three decades.

On the other hand, there are some topics—in the discussion of foreign policy, for example—for which there is no opportunity to ask about particular events on more than one occasion. But even then, we have found items on similar or related events and examined them in context. It should be clear, however, that while in most instances we are dealing with the same items over various time periods, at no time do we have the same respondents giving their opinions about those items. We argue, however, that one can compare the different cohorts over time and assume that they have remained relatively stable in their demographic characteristics. Since we deal only with the responses of the aggregate and do not examine responses of various occupational, educational, ethnic, or racial groups within the population, even the differences in sampling techniques used by the different polling agencies or the changes made over time by the same agency are not likely to lead to any serious distortions.

Norval Glenn (1970, p. 83) wrote that:

> the foremost problem with the quota samples used by Gallup, Roper, NORC [National Opinion Research Center], and the other polling organizations during the 1930s, 1940s, and early 1950s, is that they systematically underrepresented certain segments of the population. . . . the lower educational, income, and occupational levels.

But while emphasizing that "the researcher needs to be alerted to these circumstances and needs to know how to deal with them when they encounter them," Glenn concludes that "usually this neglect has led to no serious errors." And "correction for systematic error is needed only if the responses differ to an important degree among the social levels." Thus, in specific chapters where it is appropriate, we note the changes in the representativeness of the sample, for example, from the early 1950's and later. But on the whole we believe that our basic approach is sound: that one can examine responses by different individuals to the same items over time and interpret those responses as indicators of reliability. Sound, especially for the topics with which we are dealing.

A second issue, which is closely related to the matter of reliability, is that of the validity of the responses. In the context of this study, we mean by validity the likelihood that the verbal responses are proxies for behavior. Opinions in the context in which we are examining them are useful mainly because we think they tell us what the public wants and does not want of its government and, hopefully, what the public is likely to support and not support when it goes to the ballot box. But, here again, we do not have any direct way of measuring the verbal responses against the behavior adopted for any of the problems under discussion, except by analogy.

In the literature on voting, there is ample evidence that voters' verbal choices before they cast their ballots and the election results match very closely. Even in those dramatic and important instances in which the pollsters picked the wrong man to win (their choice of Dewey over Truman in 1948 and of Harold Wilson over Edward Heath in the British elections in 1970), they were off by only a few percentage points. Not since the *Literary Digest's* prediction that Alfred Landon would defeat Franklin Roosevelt in the 1936 Presidential election have the pollsters been off by more than three or four percentage points. Needless to say, in the case of these events, those few points made all the difference. But for the problems discussed here, if the opinions reported predicted behavior as well as verbal preferences for Presidential candidates predicted how the respondent was likely to vote, we would have a sense of assurance about the validity of those responses.

Another area in which the public's verbal preferences or attitudes and behavior match closely is in market research. A high proportion of the time, the products that people say they want, like, or will buy turn out to be the ones they in fact purchase. Having found a good deal of consistency between verbal expression and overt behavior in voting and consumer behavior, we believe it is just as likely that if, and when, people are given the opportunity to act on the opinions reported in this study, their behavior would also be consistent with their opinions a great majority of the time. One can therefore use their opinions about allowing their children to attend a school where a majority of the pupils are black, or being willing to go into business with a Jew, or permitting their church to be used by a "peace group" as proxies for how they would behave should an appropriate situation arise.

Two other criticisms that might be leveled against our approach are (1) that we have assumed that national surveys are the best sources for determining what the important public issues are and that we have ignored the possibility that the topics around which surveys are based are those that lend themselves most conveniently to interview situations; and (2) that they are the kinds of issues that can be asked by one stranger of another. But what of issues that do not lend themselves to such a format, and what about frankness on the part of the respondent? What assurance do we have that the respondent is not "playing the role of a respondent" and in that role is giving answers that he would not give his friends, his wife, or other persons with whom he is not as guarded?

On the first issue, concerning the decision as to what the important or significant issues are, that determination was made independently of the poll data, on the basis of a review of the history of the period. A list of topics was prepared independently of the data available from the polls, and the list was then compared against available survey data. We found, for example, that there were not enough poll data to warrant an analysis of American attitudes toward minority groups other than Jews and Negroes. Our original plan was to include Mexicans, Indians, and others. We had hoped to assess attitudes toward deviant behavior (crime, addiction, mental illness, and the like), but on this topic also there was not enough information extending over a long enough period of time. Some of the other topics for which data were available, but not in the detail and over the time we required, were matters dealing with civil liberties, population growth, and China. Some analysis, however, could be made on each of these topics. There appeared to be sufficient poll data available on the other topics that we had determined, independently, were events we wished to include in our study. We would argue, therefore, that the topics covered by the polls over a thirty-year time span do provide an adequate representation of the salient issues with which the society was confronted.

On the matter of how candid respondents are during an interview, we believe that the issues discussed in this study have public importance but do not probe too intimately into the individual's psyche. They are matters about which individuals can be honest without feeling that they are exposing their most intimate thoughts to public scrutiny or even to that of the interviewer. The frankness issue, therefore, is not germane to this study.

DATA SOURCES

The polls reported in this volume have been obtained from three main sources: the periodicals *Public Opinion Quarterly* and *Gallup Monthly Report* and the Roper Public Opinion Research Center in Williamstown, Massachusetts. From these sources we were able to obtain data from surveys run by the National Opinion Research Center, the George Gallup American Institute of Public Opinion, Louis Harris Associates, and any other major polling agencies that conducted national surveys from the late 1930's to 1970. We do not, however, claim to have analyzed all of the national surveys conducted during that period. We do have all those reported in the polls section of the *Public Opinion Quarterly* from 1937 on, and more recently from the *Gallup Monthly Report*. For specific topics, such as civil rights, aspects of foreign policy, trade unions, and social security, we wrote to the Public Opinion Research Center in Williamstown, and obtained data from them. But we have not included every item on each of the topics covered in the subsequent chapters. We have tried to use items that have been asked repeatedly or, failing that, those that we considered most salient for a particular issue. Each of the topics that is treated in a chapter or a part of a chapter could have been discussed at much greater length. In some instances, for example, in the analysis of anti-Semitism, we cite several important recent studies that have used national surveys to assess attitudes towards Jews in American society.

The typical sample size for national polls is 1,500 respondents. Pollsters claim that with a sample that size there is a ·95 probability that the results obtained are no more than three percentage points off the figure that would be obtained if every adult in the country were interviewed. They also claim that to shave even one point from the percentages that are obtained with a sample of 1,500, to come even closer to reproducing the universe, would involve tapping twice as many people. It would thus be extremely expensive and time-consuming to increase substantially the sample size, and the rewards for doing so would be minute.

A danger, particularly when one is comparing poll data over time, but even in cross-sectional analysis, is knowledge about whether a "filter question" has been used; that is, a question asked only of respondents who gave a certain response to a previous item. For example, when reporting approval or disapproval of what Senator McCarthy was doing in 1952, it is important to know whether there was an item that preceded the approval–disapproval one, which asked: "Have you heard of Senator Joseph McCarthy?" Suppose there had been, and 52 percent answered "no." Only the remaining 48 percent would then have been asked their opinion about what he was doing. And the percent who answered "yes," they approved would be based only on those 48 percent. In almost every instance, we saw the entire survey before we selected the items that were to be included in this volume. Therefore, when there were filter questions, we either reported them beforehand or acknowledged their existence in interpreting the responses to the question that followed.

In the chapters that follow, we identify the source of each question by placing the initials of the polling agency from which the item was taken. The agencies involved and the initials used to identify them are as follows:

Fortune (FOR)
George Gallup American Institute of Public Opinion (AIPO)
Louis Harris Associates (HAR)
National Opinion Research Center (NORC)
Office of Public Opinion Research (OPOR)
Roper Research Associates (ROP)
Survey Research Center, University of Michigan (SRC)

Items that were taken from published studies rather than from the polls directly have been documented accordingly.

Many writers have discussed each of the topics contained in this volume more incisively and in greater detail. Still others have written about each of the time periods covered in this volume—the depression, the war years, the postwar era—in greater depth. But the distinctive strength and usefulness of this volume is that it reports opinions on most of the major public issues involving domestic and foreign policy with which the American public and government were confronted over the entire period for which national poll data are available.

SUGGESTED READINGS

Berelson, Bernard, and Morris Janowitz. *Reader in Public Opinion and Communication.* 2nd ed.; New York, 1966.

Cantril, Hadley. *Gauging Public Opinion.* Princeton, 1947.

Doob, Leonard W. *Public Opinion and Propaganda.* New York, 1948.

Edelman, Murray. *The Symbolic Uses of Politics.* Urbana, Ill., 1964.

Glenn, Norval. "Problems of Comparability in Trend Studies with Opinion Poll Data." *Public Opinion Quarterly,* 34, No. 1 (1970), 82-91.

Katz, Daniel, *et al. Public Opinion and Propaganda.* New York, 1962.

Kornhauser, William. *The Politics of Mass Society.* Glencoe, Ill., 1959.

Lane, Robert, and David Sears. *Public Opinion.* Englewood Cliffs, N.J., 1964.

Lang, Kurt, and Gladys Lang. *Collective Dynamics.* New York, 1961.

Lippmann, Walter. *Public Opinion.* New York, 1922.

Murphy, Gardner, and Rensis Likert. *Public Opinion and the Individual.* New York, 1938.

Rogers, Lindsay. *The Pollsters: Public Opinion, Politics and Democratic Leadership.* New York, 1949.

Salomon, Ernst von. *Fragebogen (The Questionnaire).* New York, 1955.

Simon, Rita J., ed. *As We Saw the Thirties.* Urbana, Ill., 1967.

Turner, Ralph, and Lewis M. Killian. *Collective Behavior.* Englewood Cliffs, N.J., 1957.

II
MAJOR DOMESTIC ISSUES

In a democracy, there are some public issues about which all of us believe the collective opinions of the citizenry should be solicited and respected in determining public policy. Some of us may be more willing to delegate the formulation of our foreign policy to experts. Others may be more willing to allow some aspects of our domestic program—tariff or antitrust regulations, for example—to be determined largely by professionals or persons who have access to more specialized information than is available to the average citizen. But on many of the important public issues, especially those that affect the well-being of our children and families, our livelihoods and financial security, we advocate a relationship such that the legislation enacted in these areas reflects the consensus of a majority of the citizens. Indeed, if upon examination we were to find that there was no relationship between public opinion and public policy, at least in the areas mentioned, then some would argue that a crucial distinction between a democratic and a nondemocratic society had disappeared.

Many political scientists who have written about the relationship between popular sentiment and the functioning of government in democratic societies—for example, V. O. Key (1961), David Truman (1951), and John Dickinson (1930)—have argued that most policy decisions are made under circumstances in which an extremely small proportion of the general public has any awareness of the particular issue. Dickinson (1930, p. 291) claims that:

> the task of government . . . is not to express an imaginary popular will, but to effect adjustments among the various special wills and purposes which at any given time are pressing for realizations. . . . These special wills and purposes are reflected in the small cluster of opinions that develop within the larger uninformed and inattentive public.

Key (1961, p. 91) agrees essentially with Dickinson's view, that most people have no opinions or preferences on specific issues, but asks:

> What characteristics of the interaction between government and popular opinion can be invoked to convert such a condition into government by, or in accord with, mass preferences?

Key's explanation is that broad popular sentiments are *indirectly* controlling. His argument assumes that while the public may have no position on specific issues or questions of policy, vague sentiments of "fairness," "justice," and "policy propriety" are widely held within the general public, and government officials are guided by these inchoate public attitudes in deciding day-to-day questions. Key also argues that there exists between the general public and the government a "layer of political activists or influentials" (composed usually of lobbyists or heads of pressure groups or professional organizations), and this layer interacts most closely with government officials on specific matters of public policy. It is this layer of political activists that in turn influences and mobilizes public or mass opinion on crucial issues.

Given this view, with which we essentially agree, that the public is not likely to have opinions about specific details or issues involving public policy, but that it does have sentiments as to the fairness, justness, and appropriateness of governmental decisions, the strategy adopted for this volume is to report responses to issues that are of general interest and not to probe too deeply into the details of specific pieces of legislation or areas of policy.

The focus of this chapter and of the three that follow is the tracing of public opinion on some of the major issues in domestic policy from the late 1930's to the end of the 1960's. The topics discussed were chosen because poll data are available over extended periods of time and because they have the the qualities described above: namely, they concern areas of general interest that are likely to have direct and important effects on the public's day-to-day behavior. The specific topics reviewed in the present chapter concern attitudes about (1) labor unions and major legislation affecting trade unions; (2) programs dealing with welfare, health and education; (3) personal income tax; and (4) population growth and birth control. Chapters III, IV, and V review public opinion on three other important domestic issues: civil rights, anti-Semitism, and civil liberties.

TRADE UNIONS AND TRADE-UNION LEGISLATION

The survey data show that the American public has been consistent in its support of the *principle* of trade unionism over three decades—

II-1.   Percent Approving of Labor Unions, 1936-1967 (AIPO)

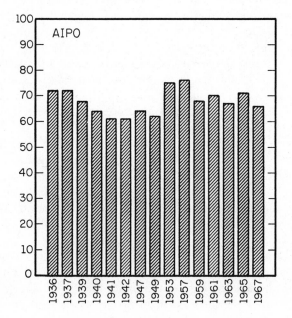

a period that encompassed a major economic depression, a world war, and peacetime affluence. The public has not, however, supported many of the practices or pressures that the movement has sought to exert on employers or on the economy generally. Graph II-1 shows the proportion who approved of labor unions from 1936 through 1967. At no time did approval drop below 61 percent, which indicates, even at that level, widespread support. The low period occurred during and after World War II, and anticipated by a few years the passage of the Taft-Hartley Act—a bill strongly opposed by organized labor, vetoed by President Truman, and popularly branded "the slave-labor act" by its opponents. Generally, we see from the figures in Graph II-1 that support, in principle, for labor unions has been widespread and steady over the past thirty years—a period marked by strong fluctuations in the nation's economy.

Additional evidence of the public's support, this time more specifically for the right of organized labor to strike, appears as Table II-1, in response to an item that asked whether or not there should be a law passed that would make it unlawful to strike during

Table II-1. Law Barring Strikes in Peacetime, 1944-1966 (AIPO)

Year	Favor	Oppose	Don't Know
1944	24%	64%	12%
1947*	28	62	10
1949*	33	55	12
1966*	27	61	12

*In 1947, 1949, and 1966, the question read: "Do you think there should or should not be a law passed that makes it unlawful to strike during peacetime under any circumstances?"

peacetime under any circumstances. Over the period of the two decades in which the item appeared on national surveys, no more than one-third of the respondents ever advocated adoption of a "no-strike policy."

The data in Graph II-1 and Table II-1 describe the public's support for a labor movement's two most basic rights: the right to organize and the right to strike. On these fundamental issues, labor unions in the United States have enjoyed consistent and widespread public approval. But at various times more specific practices that trade unions have engaged in or pressures they have sought to exert in order to obtain an advantage in a particular dispute or in periods of economic hardship have not received widespread public support, even though spokesmen for the movement have claimed that such practices were necessary for the union's existence. The "closed shop" (a shop in which the only persons hired are those who are already members of the union) and the "union shop" (a shop in which every worker who is hired must join the union) are examples of practices that trade unions have claimed were essential for their existence but which most of the public did not support, as shown in Table II-2 and Graph II-2.

Table II-2.   Closed Shop, 1937-1945 (AIPO)*

Year	Favor	Oppose	No Opinion
1937	28%	59%	13%
1939	23	62	15
1941	13	77	10
1945	13	75	12

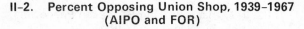

*The term "closed shop" was defined before respondents were asked for their opinion.

II-2.   Percent Opposing Union Shop, 1939-1967 (AIPO and FOR)

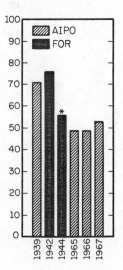

In January 1947, when the public was asked which one of the three types of shops they preferred—the closed, the union, or the open—8 percent said they favored a closed shop, 18 percent a union shop, 8 percent had no opinion, and 66 percent favored an open shop (AIPO).[1] The closed shop was declared illegal under one of the provisions of the Taft-Hartley Act that was passed about the time the 1947 item appeared and to which only 8 percent reacted favorably. Since the end of World War II, the trend, as manifested by the 66 percent who favored the open shop in 1947, and the extent of public support for right-to-work laws seem to be in the direction of favoring a decrease in the union's power over control of the labor force. In 1957, and a decade or so later in 1968, 62 and 63 percent said they would vote for a law that states each worker has the right to hold his job in a company whether he joins the labor union or not (AIPO).

In opposition to trade-union policy, the public also supports compulsory arbitration. When the issue was first raised during the depression (1937), 89 percent indicated that they favored such a practice (AIPO). By the middle 1960's, the proportion favorable was not quite as high, but as of the latest survey, as shown in Graph II-3, the ratio was still 3:1 in favor of compulsory arbitration (AIPO).[2]

We turn next to an examination of the public's responses to two major pieces of labor legislation: the first was enacted during the depression; the second during a period of affluence following World War II. The first is the Wagner[3] or National Labor Relations Act, passed in 1935 and considered by labor to be its Bill of Rights. The second is the Taft-Hartley or Labor Management Relations Act, which became law over a Presidential veto in 1947.

The Wagner Act provided many benefits to the trade-union movement. It provided for a National Labor Relations Board with power to conduct elections to determine whether employees wanted to be represented by a union. It restricted employers from unfair practices such as discharging workers for union membership, setting

[1] Each type was explained to the person interviewed.
[2] Mediation (the recommendation of which is not binding on either side) was also favored by a large proportion of the public. In 1939, 86 percent indicated their approval, and in 1945, 70 percent favored it (AIPO).
[3] Robert Wagner, Senator from New York, sponsored the bill.

**II-3. Percent Favoring Compulsory Arbitration,
1937-1968 (AIPO)**

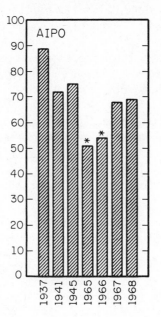

up company unions, and refusing to negotiate with union representatives in good faith.

The Taft-Hartley Act was viewed by its supporters as a much-
needed balance against the existing prolabor legislation and by its
opponents as a powerful antilabor measure. Among the more controversial provisions of the Taft-Hartley Act was that it declared the
closed shop illegal. It permitted unions to be sued for engaging in
jurisdictional disputes and secondary boycotts. It prohibited labor
from exacting pay for work not performed (featherbedding). It permitted employers to present "their side" during organizational
campaigns and to ask the National Labor Relations Board to hold
elections to determine bargaining agents. The law also made it
mandatory for union officers to sign affidavits that they were not
members of the Communist Party before the union could engage in
collective bargaining. Finally, it empowered the President to ask for
court injunctions that could forestall for 80 days a strike that in his
opinion would endanger national welfare.

Between 1938, three years after the passage of the Wagner Act, and 1952, five years after the Taft-Hartley bill was enacted into law, the public was asked on several occasions whether it thought each act should be revised, repealed, or left unchanged. The results are shown in Table II-3. On the whole, the distribution of responses to

Table II-3. Wagner and Taft-Hartley Acts, 1938-1967 (AIPO)

Year	Revise	Repeal	Leave Unchanged	No Opinion
Wagner Act				
1938	43%	19%	38%	—
1939	48	18	34	—
1967	53	11	36	—
Taft-Hartley Act				
1947	43%	28%	29%	—
1948	47	20	33	—
1949	42	23	35	—
1952*	25	17	38	20

*In 1952, the question read: "Do you think the Taft-Hartley law should be left as is, changed, or done away with?"

two pieces of legislation that evoked such sharp differences of opinion among politicians, labor leaders, and management is remarkably similar. Even in 1947, when the public had a chance to respond to both acts in the same year, the proportion who said they favored revising both bills was the modal response. It is not surprising that in that year more respondents favored repeal of the Taft-Hartley Act than of the Wagner Act. After all, 1947 was the year in which the bill was attacked most strenuously, and the attack was led by no less a person than the President of the United States. The public's response to these items should be interpreted as supporting a compromise position between what might have been thought of as the "prolabor excesses" of the Wagner Act and the "antilabor responses" that are manifest in some of the provisions of the Taft-Hartley Act.

Having examined the public's attitudes toward the Wagner and Taft-Hartley Acts on the most general dimensions of whether it favored or opposed them, we report next the public's attitudes toward a few of the provisions of the Taft-Hartley Act, to which organized labor responded with the most vehemence: the enforced observance of a "cooling-off period";[4] provisions for punishing unions engaged in jurisdictional strikes;[5] declaring featherbedding[6] illegal; and making mandatory the use of a secret ballot when a labor union asks its members whether they favor or oppose going out on strike. The public's attitudes toward each of these measures are shown in Table II-4.

Table II-4.   Provisions of Taft-Hartley Act, 1946 (AIPO)

Provision	Favor	Oppose	No Opinion
Enforced observance of cooling-off period	78%	10%	12%
Punishment for jurisdictional strikes	71	10	19
Ban of featherbedding*	60	23	17
Use of scret ballot on strike vote	84	†	†

*The public was asked its opinion about featherbedding on at least half a dozen national surveys between 1943 and 1962. The 60 percent shown above was reported for 1946, the year closest to the passage of the Taft-Hartley Act, which made the practice illegal. Before 1946, the percentage who opposed featherbedding ranged from 62 to 69. By 1959 and 1962, the public's opinion had softened somewhat, and only 54 percent opposed the practice in those years.
†Not known.

The public's support for each of these measures is clearly demonstrated in the table. Public support for the Taft-Hartley Act was also indirectly demonstrated by the fact that in the elections that were held in 1950, Senator Robert Taft was easily reelected to the Senate from the heavily industrialized and unionized state of Ohio. We note also that prior to passage of the Taft-Hartley Act, when the public was asked in 1946 (a period marked by strikes in major industries) whether the government ought to take "a strong hand in labor strikes" and whether it ought to pass new laws to control labor unions, 74 and 66 percent answered "yes" to each question.

[4]This is a period before a union can carry out its intention to strike in a major industry and during which a committee appointed by the government examines the cause of the dispute and makes public its report.
[5]A jurisdictional strike is a situation in which employees who belong to a different union strike over which union has the right to perform a job.
[6]Featherbedding is a practice of making jobs for union members by requiring employers to hire more men than are actually needed to do a particular job in order to provide work for all their members.

Later evidence that the public continued to support restricting organized labor's activities may be found in responses to items that appeared on national polls at least four times between 1961 and 1966. The items differed only in the object about which the public's evaluation was sought. The results described in Table II-5 show that in the middle 1960's about twice as many respondents believed that the laws regulating labor as opposed to business were "not strict enough." Between 1962 and 1966, there was an increase in the

Table II-5. Strictness of Laws Regulating Unions and Businesses, 1961–1966 (AIPO)

Year	Too Strict		Not Strict Enough		About Right		Don't Know	
	Labor	Business	Labor	Business	Labor	Business	Labor	Business
1961	9%	9%	42%	26%	27%	32%	22%	33%
1962	10	13	48	27	25	29	17	31
1965	10	18	42	21	27	32	21	29
1966	11	20	40	20	25	32	24	28

percentage who believed that the laws regulating business were "too strict" and a comparable decline in the percentage who thought that they were "not strict enough." The percent supporting labor, on the other hand, remained relatively stable over the five-year period. These opinions, we note, were solicited in the last few years, not in the immediate postwar era when labor engaged in strikes in major industries for which they were accused by many public officials of disrupting the nation's economy at a time when major industries were in the process of converting from war to peacetime production.[7]

We conclude this review of public opinion toward organized labor by reemphasizing the observations made at the outset. In principle, more of the public favors trade unions (at least it favors

[7] In the 1950's the same item was asked about labor with the following results (AIPO):

Year	Too Strict	Not Strict Enough	About Right	No Opinion or No Answer
1952	12%	38%	26%	24%
1953	10	33	37	20
1954	6	49	20	25

the right of workers to organize and to bargain collectively) than oppose them.[8] But the public has opposed many of the objectives that labor sought to achieve over the past thirty years and has urged government intervention against unions during crucial periods. Especially in the immediate postwar era the public's mood was supportive of acts that curbed the power of organized labor. Not only did it not oppose the general tenor of the Taft-Hartley Act, but it strongly supported some of the sections of the bill that labor most vehemently opposed. In the twenty years since the end of World War II, the public has moderated its views somewhat, but it still opposes many of the objectives that organized labor has declared itself in favor of most ardently; and in more recent polls the public appears more punitive toward organized labor than toward business.

SOCIAL-WELFARE LEGISLATION

Old-Age Pensions and Social Security

In contrast to the public's ambivalence or negative attitude toward some practices or aspects of trade unionism, it has manifested stronger and more consistent approval for most major pieces of social-welfare legislation. Old-age pensions and social security have received the most widespread and consistent support. Paul Douglas, former Professor of Economics and Senator from Illinois, wrote in the first sentence of his comprehensive analysis of the then recently enacted social-security legislation (Douglas, 1936, p. 3):

> the federal security act is the result of a very sharp change in public opinion. Prior to the great depression, the consensus of public opinion was that American citizens could in the main provide for their own old age by individual savings. So far as unemployment was concerned, the articulate American public predominantly believed either that unemployment was being reduced to very narrow limits by "the stabilization of industry" or that unemployment insurance was a debasing "dole" which subsidized men for being idle and hence led them to shun work.

[8] In 1947, the public was asked: "Do you think that an employer should or should not be required by law to bargain collectively with whatever union is elected by the majority of his workers?" The responses were distributed as follows: Should, 45%; Should not, 31%; No opinion. 24% (FOR).

In January 1936, which was shortly before the passage of a program of social security, the public was asked whether it favored government old-age pensions for needy persons, and 89 percent answered "yes" (AIPO).

On August 18, 1936, President Roosevelt signed into law the Federal Social Security Act that provided "for the general welfare by establishing a system of Federal Old Age benefits" and enabled "the several states to make more adequate provision for aged persons, blind persons, dependent and crippled children, maternal and child welfare, public health."

Between 1936 and 1940 the public was asked on several occasions whether it supported government-financed old-age pensions. Each time, between 90 and 94 percent answered that it did (AIPO). In 1939, 87 percent indicated that it would be willing to pay a sales tax or an income tax to provide for old-age pensions (AIPO).

After World War II (in 1947), the issue posed was the extension of social-security benefits to groups not previously covered.[9] When the public was asked whether it wanted social security extended so that more people would get payments under it, changed so that fewer people would get payments, or left about as it was, the responses were distributed as follows (FOR):

More	Fewer	Left As Is	Other	No Opinion
48%	3%	32%	3%	14%

The public's willingness to extend social-security benefits was consistent with its previous responses (in 1938 and 1943) when 74 and 64 percent respectively, indicated a willingness to extend benefits to household help, farm hands, and employees in small shops (AIPO).

In his address to the Democratic Convention in July 1948, President Truman chastised the Congress for its failure to extend social-security payments (quoted in Bernstein and Matusow, 1966, pp. 151–152):

> Time and again I have recommended improvements in the social security Law, including extending protection to those not now covered, and increasing the amount of benefits to reduce the eligibility age of women from 65 to 60 years. Congress studied the matter for two years but

[9]Under the original act, persons employed in agricultural labor, domestic service, casual labor, and government employees were not covered.

could not find the time to increase the benefits. But they did find the time to take social security benefits away from 750,000 people, and they passed that over my veto.

In the 1950's the public was asked:

> Under the present law, a person 65 years of age who receives social-security benefits has to give them up if he holds a job and earns more than $50 a month. Do you approve or disapprove of this (AIPO)?

Table II-6.   Social Security for Person Earning More Than $50 a Month, 1952-1959 (AIPO)

Year	Favor	Oppose	No Opinion
1952	19%	74%	7%
1959*	22	68	10

*In 1959, the question read: "A person over 65 who works full-time and earns more than $1200 a year cannot receive social-security payments. Do you think this law should or should not be changed?"

The responses, shown in Table II-6, indicate that on this issue public opinion was ahead of government policy, even the policy of the Democratic administration, which was more liberal on these matters than were the Republicans alluded to in Truman's speech at the 1948 Democratic Convention. The public wished to have social security extended to include persons over 65 in the labor force who earned more significant sums of money.

Some indication of how far the public was willing to go in its interpretation of social-security and old-age benefits may be seen from the responses to the following items that were asked in the 1940's:

> Do you think the government should provide for all people who have no other means of obtaining a living (FOR)?

In 1940, 65 percent and in 1947, 73 percent answered "yes." In 1943, they were asked:

> Do you think a "cradle to grave" program of minimum security for all people in the United States is _____ (FOR)?
>
> Impossible and undesirable   44%
> Economically possible but undesirable   15
> Desirable but impossible   21
> Economically possible and desirable   20

Responses to both items indicate that most people supported the practice of government aid to old people who are unable to provide for themselves. But the principle that the government should automatically provide for those beyond a productive age was rejected by most people on economic as well as moral grounds.

Medical Programs

We now shift from social security to government-sponsored medical programs and assess the level of public support in that sphere. Unlike social-security benefits, minimum-wage and maximum-hour controls, regulations protecting women and children in the labor force, and benefits to farmers, neither the New Deal under Franklin Roosevelt nor the Fair Deal under Harry Truman nor the New Frontier of the Kennedy administration succeeded in passing a government-sponsored medical program. It was not until 1965, under President Johnson's blueprint for a Great Society, that a massive government-sponsored health-care bill was enacted. In the late 1930's (during the depression) and during the war, the public supported such a program, but in the years immediately following World War II such proposals experienced a sharp decline in public approval. It was not until the beginning of the 1960's that public attitudes shifted again, in a more positive direction.

In 1938, 81 percent answered "yes," the government should be responsible for providing medical care for people who are unable to pay for it (AIPO). Moreover, 59 percent said they would be willing to pay higher taxes to support such a program (AIPO). Four years later, which was during the war, the public continued to support a government-sponsored medical program. When asked which programs the federal government should collect enough taxes for after the war, 74 percent felt that "medical care for everyone who needs it" should be one of the programs (FOR). In 1943, 59 percent favored extending the social-security program to include payments for sickness, disability, physicians' fees, and hospital bills (AIPO).[10]

The first signs that public opinion had shifted away from support of some sort of comprehensive government-sponsored medical-care program appeared in 1946. When asked the following question,

---

[10] Social security provided benefits for old age, death, and unemployment.

responses were in the order of preference listed below:

> What do you think should be done, if anything, to
> provide for the payment of doctor, dental, and hospital
> bills for people in this country (AIPO)?
>
> | | |
> |---|---|
> | *a.* Nothing | 25% |
> | *b.* Voluntary health insurance, Blue Cross, etc. | 17 |
> | *c.* Medical insurance under social security | 12 |
> | *d.* Special grants for hospitals and clinics | 11 |
> | *e.* Private or community charity | 6 |
> | *f.* Miscellaneous | 12 |
> | *g.* Don't know | 16 |

Those who favored doing nothing about the problem or who advocated relying upon private and voluntary sources (a combination of categories *a, b,* and *e*) amounted to 49 percent. Only 12 percent recommended a program of medical insurance under social security.

In a special message to the Congress, shortly after his election in 1948, President Truman recommended a Comprehensive Health Program, at the heart of which was a proposal for compulsory national health insurance. In that message, Truman said (quoted in Bernstein and Matusow, 1966, pp. 115-116):

> We should resolve now that the health of this Nation is a
> national concern; that financial barriers in the way of
> attaining health shall be removed; that the health of all
> its citizens deserves the help of all the nation . . . the
> principal reason why people do not receive the care they
> need is that they cannot afford to pay for it on an
> individual basis at the time they need it. This is true not
> only for needy persons. It is also true for a large propor-
> tion of normally self supporting persons . . . I recommend
> solving the basic problem by distributing the costs
> through expansion of our existing compulsory social
> insurance system.

The public was polled a few weeks after Truman's message and asked whether it supported the President's health-insurance scheme. Only 56 percent claimed to have any familiarity with the proposed legislation (AIPO). Among them, the proportions were evenly divided: 38 percent favored the plan, and 38 percent opposed it. The remaining 24 percent had no opinion.

Given a choice between the Truman administration's bill and a plan proposed by the American Medical Association (each was explained briefly), the AMA's private voluntary program received almost one and a half times as much support: Truman plan, 33%; AMA plan, 47%; Neither, 7%; No opinion, 3% (AIPO).

A year later, when the same item was asked again, the distribution of responses was almost identical to that of the previous year.

Some explanation for the public's lack of support may be found in its beliefs about the quality of the medical care that would be available under a government-sponsored health-insurance program. When asked specifically about the quality of services they associated with a government health program, the responses were as shown in Table II-7. In 1946, 55 percent thought that the care provided under

Table II-7.   Quality of Care under Government versus Private Health Plan, 1946–1949 (AIPO)

Year	Better	Same	Not as Good	No Opinion
1946	32%	23%	35%	10%
1949	26	19	43	12

a government-sponsored program would be better than or the same quality as they were receiving at the time. One-third thought that it would not be as good. Three years later, when debate over the administration's program was at its height, the proportion who believed it would not be as good, increased and the "better" and "same" categories declined slightly, so that among the respondents with an opinion there was about a fifty-fifty split. But expectations about the quality of the medical care they would receive under a government-sponsored program does not fully explain the public's lack of support for the Truman proposal.

The strongest organized opponent of the administration's bill was the American Medical Association. In its attack, the AMA emphasized the "political" overtures of such a program. For example, an editorial that appeared on January 15, 1949, in the *Journal of the American Medical Association* stated:

> The Congress, if it should adopt any considerable number of the recommendations made, would move the nation away from its present status as a republic or a true democracy into a condition which resembles what is called in Europe a socialist democracy.

Respondents who favored the AMA's voluntary plan, as opposed to the compulsory insurance advocated by President Truman, were undoubtedly responding positively to the AMA's warning that adoption of the voluntary program would be a significant step forward to ward off socialism.

After the administration's bills were defeated in the Congress, a dozen years passed before the public was asked again on any national survey for its opinion of a medical-insurance program that would be administered under social security. By that time, public opinion had shifted again, in favor of a national compulsory insurance plan. The data in Table II-8 describe the level of public support between 1961 and 1965 for such a plan.

Table II-8.   Medical-Insurance Plan under Social Security, 1961-1965 (AIPO)

Year	Favor	Oppose	No Opinion
1961	67%	26%	7%
1964	58	31	11
1965	63	28	9

The Truman plan proposed in 1949 and the Medicare program advocated by President Johnson in 1965 had many basic similarities. But it took almost twenty years from the time the plan was first seriously debated by the Congress, in 1949, until its adoption in 1965. By the time it was adopted, public opinion was behind it (AIPO).

Minimum-Wage Standards

We turn the clock back again to the 1930's and trace public support for another major piece of social-welfare legislation: the adoption of a minimum-wage standard to be paid to all persons working in industries engaged in interstate commerce. Before the Fair Labor Standards Act of 1938 was adopted, in which 25 cents per hour was established as the minimum wage that could be paid, the public was asked whether it thought the federal government ought to set such standards, and 61 percent said "yes" (AIPO). Three months after the Fair Labor Standards Act was passed, the public was asked whether it favored the new law and 69 percent said it did (AIPO).

However, on the issue of what the minimum wage ought to be, the public's mean response was 40 cents per hour, compared to the government's enacted 25 cents (AIPO). In 1945, the public was polled again on the matter of determining what the minimum hourly wage should be, and the median response was 60 cents (AIPO).[11] The public was also asked whether it favored making the minimum wage 65 cents an hour; 56 percent favored that rate and 32 percent opposed it (AIPO). Between 1946 and 1949, when the minimum wage was still 40 cents an hour, the public was asked whether it approved of raising the minimum from 40 to 75 cents an hour.[12] As the figures in Table II-9 show, at least two-thirds approved of the proposed raise (AIPO).

Table II-9. Minimum Wage of 75¢ an Hour, 1946-1949 (AIPO)

Year	Favor	Oppose	No Opinion
1946	66%	26%	8%
1947	71	24	5
1948	66	29	5
1949	66	29	5

In the 1950's, when the minimum hourly wage was at first 75 cents an hour and then raised to $1.00, the public was asked whether the amount should be raised and it responded as shown in Table II-10.

Table II-10. Minimum Wage of $1.00 and $1.25 an Hour, 1953-1957 (AIPO)

Year	Favor	Oppose	No Opinion
1953*	59%	33%	8%
1954 †	60	36	4
1957 †	66	28	6

*Raise to $1.00.
†Raise to $1.25.

In 1966, the minimum hourly wage was raised to $1.60. When the public was asked its opinion about what the minimum wage

[11] By 1945, the minimum hourly wage had been raised to 40 cents.
[12] In 1949, the minimum hourly wage, effective January 1950, was set at 75 cents an hour.

should be in September 1965, 55 percent favored an immediate increase, 39 percent believed it should be left as it was for the next year or two, and 6 percent had no opinion.

In each instance, we note that the public strongly and consistently supported the principle of a minimum hourly wage. Over the past thirty years, it has also consistently anticipated government decisions about what the minimum standard should be and has advocate a higher wage than that currently established by law.

A major plank in the policy recommendations of the civil-rights movement, when led by the Reverend Martin Luther King, Jr., organized labor, and the left wing of the Democratic Party, has been legislation favoring a guaranteed annual income. Daniel Moynihan, in his capacity as Special Advisor to President Nixon, urged that much of the current welfare program be scrapped in favor of direct financial payment to persons who are unable to work or whose income is less than a certain minimum. The minimum would be determined by size of family, age of children, and the like. At this writing, such legislation has not been adopted, but it has received support not only from the groups mentioned above but from persons in government and at universities who perceive themselves as adherents of the classical school of economics and who tend on political issues to vote with the more conservative elements within the Republican Party.

For the first time in October 1965, the public was asked, on a national poll, to react to the proposal that the government provide a family with a minimal annual income. The specific item and the distribution of responses are shown below:

> It has been proposed that instead of relief and welfare payments, the government should guarantee every family a minimum annual income. Do you favor or oppose this idea (AIPO)?

In response, 19 percent said they favored the idea, 14 percent had no opinion, and two-thirds opposed the plan. Three years later the public had a chance to respond to a more specific proposal. The issue posed in June 1968 and then again in January 1969 read as follows:

> As you may know, there is talk about getting every family an income of at least $3,200 a year, which would

be the amount for a family of four. If the family earns less than this, the government would make up the difference. Would you favor or oppose such a plan (AIPO)?

The results are shown in Table II-11. While the proportion who approved increased by almost 100 percent since 1965, there were still about twice as many who opposed as favored the proposal.

A program that did gain public support was one in which the government would guarantee employment, rather than direct financial subsidy, to families whose income was below the $3,200 minimum set for a family of four. When asked the following question during this same period (June 1968 and January 1969), the public was overwhelmingly favorable, as shown in Table II-11.

Table II-11. Government-Guaranteed Income and Employment, 1968–1969 (AIPO)

Month and Year	Income			Employment		
	Favor	Oppose	No Opinion	Favor	Oppose	No Opinion
June 1968	36%	58%	6%	78%	18%	4%
January 1969	32	62	6	79	16	5

Another proposal is to guarantee enough work so that each family that has an employable wage earner be guaranteed enough work each week to give him a wage of about $60 a week, or $3,200 a year. Would you favor or oppose such a plan (AIPO)?

Two and a half years later, in July 1971, another program that also emphasized providing work for persons on welfare as opposed to the existing welfare payments or direct financial subsidies received considerable public support:

It has been suggested that large companies (those employing more than 20 persons) be required to hire a certain small percentage of persons who are now on relief. In return, the government would pay three-quarters of the salary of these persons for the first year. Companies that hire persons from the welfare rolls would give them any work available and at the going wage for their jobs. If they refuse to accept this work, they would lose their welfare payments. Would you like to have the government adopt this plan or not (AIPO)?

Yes	No	No Opinion
67%	27%	6%

Federal Aid to Education

Federal aid to education, like federal support for medical care, was another major piece of welfare legislation that needed at least two and a half decades of debate and persuasion before enactment. During the second term of President Roosevelt's New Deal, in 1938, an item pertaining to federal aid to public and/or parochial schools appeared on a national survey. As the figures below indicate, 53 percent favored federal aid only to public schools and half as many favored granting federal funds to parochial schools as well:

Should federal aid be given to public and parochial schools, or should this aid be given to public schools only (AIPO)?

Public	Public and Parochial	No Opinion
53%	35%	12%

When we remember that the year was 1938, that the country was in the midst of a depression, and that it was only ten years after the 1928 Presidential campaign in which anti-Catholic feelings were intense, 35 percent seems quite high.

Following the end of World War II, the issue of federal aid to education had two major aspects. The first was tied to the problem of improving the standards of Negro education in the South under a segregated school system. The second focused on the issue of federal support for parochial schools. The Truman administration based its claim on the need for federal intervention on a large scale primarily on the first point. A report issued by President's Committee on Civil Rights in 1947 (reprinted 1967, p. 65) claimed that:

In spite of the improvement which is undoubtedly taking place, the Committee is convinced that the gap between white and Negro schools can never be completely eliminated by means of state funds alone. The cost of maintaining separate but truly equal, school systems would seem to be utterly prohibitive in many of the southern states. It seems probable that the only means by which such a goal can finally be won will be through federal financial assistance. The extension of the federal grant-in-aid for educational purposes, already available to the land-grant colleges and, for vocation education, to the secondary school field, seems both imminent and desirable.

Whether the federal grant-in-aid should be used to support the maintenance of separate schools is an issue that the country must soon face.

Between 1948 (shortly after the President's Committee on Civil Rights made public its report) and 1965, the following item appeared on at least five national surveys:

There is a bill now before Congress which asks that the federal government distribute about 300 million dollars a year to the states for school aid. Do you think that Congress should provide money for this purpose, or should school aid be left entirely to the states (AIPO)?

The data in Table II-12 show that between 1948 and 1955, support for federal aid to education increased steadily. The question posed was:

Should Congress provide money for public-school aid, or should school aid be left entirely to the states (AIPŌ)?

Table II-12.   Federal Aid to Public Schools, 1948-1965 (AIPO)

Year	Yes	Qualified Yes	No	No Opinion
1948	51%	5%	31%	13%
1949	64	—	26	10
1950	65	—	24	11
1955	67	—	23	10
1965*	49	—	42	9

*In 1965, the question read: "Should the federal government pay more of these costs, or should the state and local communities continue as at present to meet almost all educational expenses for the public schools?"

But perhaps as the public realized the significance of the 1954 Supreme Court decision that declared segregated schools illegal, its willingness to have the federal government intervene financially cooled—as witness the reversal of that trend in 1965. Persons who favored a segregated school system must have realized by 1965 that there would be a better chance to stymie the Court's directive if federal financial aid were kept at a minimum and the major burden left to the states.[13] Also the issue of "states' rights" had stronger ideological overtones after the Court's decision than it had in the previous decade. When faced with the choice of federal or state intervention irrespective of the substantive issue, a sizable portion of the public would be likely to respond in favor of the states.

During the same period, the public had an opportunity to express its views on the more specific issue of whether federal aid should be provided to schools that failed to integrate white and Negro students following the 1954 decision. In Table II-13, we note

Table II-13.   Federal Aid to All or Only Integrated Schools, 1956-1961 (AIPO)

Year	All	Only Integrated	No Opinion
1956	61%	32%	7%
1957	73	17	10
1961	68	23	9

that as of 1961, the ratio was 3:1 in favor of aiding all schools, including those operating on a segregated basis.[14] The 68 percent who favored providing federal aid to all schools matches closely the percentage on a Harris poll, conducted two years later, who supported providing federal funds to public as well as parochial schools.

The other major controversy in the issue of federal aid to education centered on parochial schools. Should federal aid be limited only to the public schools, or should it be extended to include private parochial institutions? In 1938, 35 percent said they supported federal aid to parochial schools (AIPO). The issue lay dormant during the period of World War II. In 1949, when federal aid to education was again debated in the Congress, largely under the impetus of Truman's Fair Deal program, an item pertaining to it appeared on a national survey:

[13] Unfortunately, we could find no item after 1955 and earlier than 1965 to test this idea.

[14] As of 1970, the government appears to have adopted a similar position, since only about 5 percent of all the school districts have been refused federal aid because of failure to desegregate even though the Civil Rights Act of 1964 forbids federal aid to any segregated institution.

If the bill in Congress is passed, which would give 300 million dollars in aid to schools in the poorer states, should this money go entirely to public schools, or should part of it go to parochial schools (AIPO)?

Table II-14.   Federal Aid to Public and Parochial Schools, 1938-1970 (AIPO)

Year	Public	Public and Parochial	No Opinion
1938	53%	35%	12%
1949	49	41	10
1961	57	36	7
1963	44	49	7
1970	44	48	8

Table II-14 describes the results. In the twenty-five years that elapsed between 1938 and 1963, public attitudes shifted in favor of federal aid to parochial schools from 35 to 49 percent. But we note that two years earlier the percent who favored federal aid to parochial schools was almost the same as it was in 1938. Thus, the shift in attitudes occurred in the most recent two years between 1961 and 1963. It was during this period that the issue was more thoroughly and openly debated in the Congress than it had been previously. But it was also during this period that President Kennedy announced his opposition to federal support for parochial schools. In his message to the Congress, the President said that no general school-aid funds should be allocated for private schools "in accordance with the clear prohibition of the Constitution" (*Congressional Quarterly Almanac*, Vol. 10, p. 280).

The Congress in 1965 passed a bill providing federal aid to parochial as well as public schools (under certain specific conditions). In 1970, a Gallup poll included the following item:

Do you favor or oppose giving some government money to help parochial schools (AIPO)?

Favor	*Oppose*	*No Opinion*
48%	44%	8%

The results were almost identical to those reported in 1963.

PERSONAL INCOME TAX

This discussion of the public's responses to the federal income tax
is limited to a reporting of the public's attitudes on the fairness
and/or appropriateness of given tax levels. It does not report
opinions about the legitimacy of the tax on personal income, the
desirability of personal income versus other forms of taxation, or
the mechanism for collecting the tax.

Beginning in 1938, some indication of the public's attitudes
about the level of income above which a person should be expected
to pay taxes and what the appropriate tax ought to be at various
income levels is shown by the responses to the following items.

1. Do you think a single man earning less than $1,000 a
   year should be required to pay a federal income tax
   (AIPO)?
   Response: 87 percent answered "no."

2. Do you think a married man earning less than $2,500 a
   year should be required to pay a federal income tax
   (AIPO)?
   Response: 80 percent answered "no."

3. How much do you think a married man with two
   children pays in federal and state income taxes
   combined (AIPO)?
   Response: See Table II-15.

The pattern shown was repeated almost every time this question
was asked, from the end of the 1930's through the 1960's. The
public consistently *underestimates* the amount of money paid in
taxes by persons earning $10,000 or more a year. The public's
standard of how much the person *ought* to pay is also considerably
lower than the amount required by law. For income that is less than
$10,000, the public is reasonably accurate as to the proportion paid
in taxes. But there is no consistent trend between how much the
public thinks ought to be paid and the amount actually paid in the
under-$10,000 category. It is only in the higher-income categories
that the public consistently errs by underestimating the amount that
is actually paid or that should be paid to the government. The data
in Table II-15 describe the pattern.

Table II–15.   Estimate and Actual Income Tax, 1938–1961 (AIPO)

Head of Family of Four Earns	Public Thinks He Pays	Public Thinks He Should Pay	He Actually Pays
1938			
$ 5,000	$ 100	$ 150	$ 90
10,000	400	500	590
100,000	9,000	9,000	40,000
1941			
$ 3,000	$ 30	$ 60	$ 0
5,000	100	200	130
10,000	300	600	720
100,000	5,000	10,000	46,000
1947			
$ 3,000	$ 200	$ 50	$ 131
10,000	1,000	900	1,720
50,000	9,000	2,500	24,000
1949			
$ 2,500	$ 54	*	$ 0
5,000	340	*	350
50,000	5,400	*	16,000
1961			
$ 3,000	*	$ 46	$ 65
5,000	*	216	420
10,000	*	617	1,372
50,000	*	7,250	18,294
100,000	*	25,000	51,192

*In 1949 and 1961, this choice was not given.

Instead of a question about appropriate taxes for given income levels, the following item was asked:

> Do you consider the amount of federal income tax which you (your husband) have to pay as too high, too low, or about right (AIPO)?

The responses are shown in Graph II-4. The period between 1944 and 1945 is atypical. During World War II, the payment of taxes was viewed by the public as a patriotic duty. But in no year after 1949 did more Americans think that the amount they were asked to pay in taxes was "about right" compared to those who

II-4.   Percent Considering Income Tax About Right, 1944-1967 (AIPO)

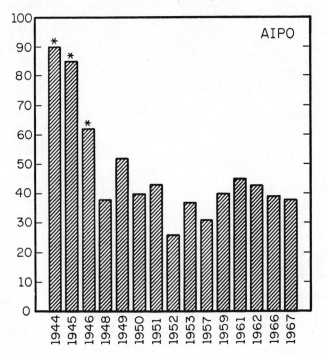

answered "too high." Neither the Korean War nor the Vietnam conflict awakened a sense of national emergency or mobilization that extended as far as the taxpayers' pocketbooks.

When asked directly and in the absence of any alternatives, the public is consistent in its belief that the amount of taxes it is asked to pay is either "too high" or "about right," and hardly ever "too low." Nevertheless, when given a choice between "balancing the federal budget" or "arming for national defense" by increasing taxes and not striving to do so (thereby retaining present tax levels), most respondents opt for balancing the budget or arming for national defense. The data shown in Table II-16 describe public reponses to proposals for changes in personal income-tax levels from 1947 through 1970.

**Table II-16.   Changes in Income-Tax Levels, 1947-1970
(FOR and AIPO)**

Item		Response		
1. Do you think that personal taxes for the coming year should be _____ (FOR)?		*1947*	*1948*	
	Reduced greatly	19%	30%	
	Reduced a little	45	40	
	Raised	1	1	
	Left as they are	26	26	
	No opinion	9	3	
2. Do you think income taxes should or should not be increased next year (AIPO)?		*1949*		
	Should not	75%		
	Should	13		
	No opinion	12		
3. Some people say federal income taxes must be increased immediately to pay for the present war in Korea and to rearm the United States. Do you agree or disagree (AIPO)?		*1950*		
	Disagree	29%		
	Agree	51		
	No opinion	20		
4. If Congress finds that it cannot balance the budget for this year and at the same time reduce income taxes, which do you think it should try to do first (AIPO)?		*1953*	*1956*	*1962*
	Cut taxes	26%	43%	19%
	Balance the budget	67	49	72
	No opinion	7	8	9
5. Have you read or heard about the Kennedy proposal to reduce income taxes [*Those who were informed were asked:*] How do you yourself feel? Do you favor or oppose a cut in income taxes now (AIPO)?		*1963*		
	Favor	60%		
	Oppose	29		
	No opinion	11		
6. President Johnson has asked Congress to pass a bill that would increase personal income taxes. If passed, it would mean that for		*1967*	*1968*	
	Reject	72%	79%	
	Pass	18	14	
	No opinion	10	7	

Table II-16.   Changes in Income-Tax Levels, 1947-1970
(FOR and AIPO)—*continued*

Item	Response	
every $100 now paid in income taxes, there would be an additional 10 percent surcharge. Should Congress reject or pass this bill (AIPO)?		
7. Suppose the local public schools said they needed much more money. As you feel at this time, would you vote to raise taxes for this purpose, or would you vote against raising taxes for this purpose (AIPO)?	For Against No opinion	*1970* 37% 56 7

Every year that the issue of a tax increase was considered, a large majority of the public opposed the proposal or indicated that they favored a reduction in taxes, except when the item made explicit reference to how the increased revenues would be used. On two out of three of those occasions, the public supported a tax increase. The choices were balancing the budget, national defense, and education. On the first two issues, the public supported a tax increase; on the education issue the public opposed a tax increase. It could be that the public would be more or less enthusiastic about other areas to which tax revenues might be applied. Perhaps the space program would rank as high as, or higher than, a balanced budget; greater input into welfare might not have as much support. There is enough evidence from the data presented to conclude that it would be a mistake to predict that the public is always opposed to increasing its tax burden. The public does not respond to the issue that way. Only when the choice between a tax increase and some other priority is *not* indicated explicitly can one predict that the public will consistently oppose a tax increase. We suspect that responses on this topic may represent universal or near-universal public attitudes irrespective of the particular society or culture in which the issue is posed.

POPULATION GROWTH AND BIRTH CONTROL

More than any other topic involving domestic affairs, perhaps with the exception of civil rights, discussions of population growth and control have been marked by the greatest shift in emphasis and concern during the period covered in this volume. In the 1930's, the concern over population focused on its decline, and policy questions centered around schemes for encouraging women to have more children. Economists and demographers saw the decreasing rate of population growth especially in the United States and in Western Europe as having a direct and negative impact on the depressed economies of those societies.

A generation later the pendulum has swung full tilt, and today biologists are warning that unless population growth is slowed or halted, civilization will be destroyed. Paul Ehrlich, the author of *The Population Bomb* (1968) and a reputable biologist, asserts that the world's food supply and other natural resources cannot and will not be able to sustain world population at its present rate of growth. Some economists, especially those associated with Resources for the Future, like Landsberg and his associates (1964), do not believe in Professor Ehrlich's prophecy of doom. They contend that there are enough natural resources or that ways will be found to develop more resources—as witness the "green revolutions" that have occurred already in parts of Asia—and that societies are not on the verge of mass destruction.

In reviewing the data available from national surveys between the late 1930's and the end of the 1960's, we found that until 1948 there were only a few items on the issue of population. And these few were concerned primarily with attitudes toward programs that might *increase* the number of children some groups in the population would be willing to have and with assessing ideal family size. From 1948 to 1965, there were no national surveys that either focused on the topic of population or included specific items. After 1965, national pollsters devoted much time to researching public opinion on this issue. We begin first with data available for the earlier period.

Between 1936 and 1948, the public was asked on at least half a dozen surveys:

> What is the ideal size of a family (husband, wife, and how many children (AIPO)?

Table II-17.   Ideal Family Size, 1936-1948 (AIPO)

Year	Two*	Three	Four	Five	Six	More Than Six	Other
1936	32%	32%	22%	14%	—	—	—
1938 †	—	—	45	28	16	—	11
1941	32	27	27	6	8	—	—
1945	23	28	31	9	9	—	—
1947	—	1	26	26	29	12	6
1948 †	1	1	32	31	23	6	6

*That is, no children.
†In 1938 and 1948, the question read: "What in your opinion is the ideal number of children in a family?" In the other years, the question referred to the total number of persons in a family.

Table II-17 describes the responses for the entire period. We note that between 1936 and 1941, one-third of the respondents answered "no children," and an additional 27-32 percent said "one child."[15] By 1948, the proportions that favored "no children" or "one child" had all but disappeared. But as late as 1945, those two categories still accounted for 51 percent of the responses. In 1948, one-third of the respondents thought "two children" comprised the ideal family size, and another third answered "three children."[16]

In 1941, when the public was asked what it thought the main reasons were that couples did not have more children, 62 percent answered "the cost of living," "we do not have enough money," and "economic uncertainty about the future" (AIPO). Lee Rainwater (1960) quotes lower-class husbands and wives saying "we cannot afford to have more children" as the main reason for their practicing or desiring to practice birth control in 1960.

Immediately after World War II, questions about the following plans appeared on a national poll:

1. *To encourage having children,* England now pays $1.00 per week for each child under 16 years of age. Do you think we should have a baby bonus of that type in this country (AIPO)?

[15] Donald Bogue (1961, pp. 137, 681) reported that during the depression, the United States had grown more slowly than at any time in its history. Total fertility was only slightly above two children per completed family.

[16] By 1948, the crude birth rate had reached a high point of 26.5 per thousand. It had not been this high since 1920-1921, the year following World War I (Bogue, 1961, p. 138).

2. *To help parents support their children,* England now pays $1.00 a week for each child under 16 years of age. Do you think we should have a baby-bonus plan of that type in this country (AIPO)?

To the first item, 30 percent answered that they supported a program of financial incentives to have children, 61 percent were opposed, and 9 percent had no opinion. To the second, 6 percent said they favored such a plan, 49 percent opposed it, and 13 percent had no opinion. Providing monetary incentives for having children or for having more children did not have popular support in this country, and such a plan was never seriously considered in the 1940's and 1950's by the Congress. President Truman, for example, never included such an idea in any of his Fair Deal programs and made no proposals on this topic in any of his messages to the Congress. The relative amounts of income tax that families of differing sizes have to pay were then, and are today, the major form in which American society rewards or punishes adults that bear children.

Items concerning the dispensation of information about birth control appeared on national surveys during this early period. In December of 1936, the public was asked whether the distribution of information on birth control should be made legal; 70 percent answered "yes" (AIPO). Three years later, in January 1940, the question was asked again, with the following variation:

Would you approve or disapprove of having government health clinics furnish birth-control information to married people who want it (AIPO.?

For the over-all population the proportion who answered "yes" increased to 77 percent. When respondents were divided according to age, 85 percent of those under 30 said "yes." In the postwar period the same item appeared on several national polls. Each time, as the figures in Graph II-5 indicate, the idea was supported by a large majority of the respondents. In 1968, 70 percent indicated that they were also in favor of the United States government "helping other nations who ask our aid in their birth control program" (AIPO).

We turn now to the present period, to an era of economic affluence and population expansion. It is also an era in which some experts warn of the gravest dangers to civilization as a result of the

II-5.   Percent Favoring Distribution of Birth-Control Information, 1936-1968 (AIPO)

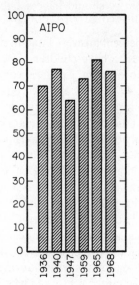

rapid growth in population and in which we see the formation of organizations such as Zero Population Growth. In discussing the implications of the population upsurge, Bogue (1961, p. 143) comments that:

1. the United States has become so large that small differences in the birthrate can provide very large differences in the population size in only a few years.
2. If the United States population growth is to be slowed down to a point where numbers remain nearly stationary or increase only gradually, birthrates must fall to a point much lower than those that prevailed since 1946. Unless this happens the annual increments to the national population will be very large.

The question for us is: How interested and concerned is the American public about population growth?

In the Summer 1967 issue of *Public Opinion Quarterly*, the polls section reproduced a survey on "population explosion and birth control" that appeared in *Look* magazine as part of a larger survey entitled "The Mood of America 1965: A National Study." The lead-off item on that survey was:

> Have you read or heard about the increase in population which is predicted for the world during the next few years?

The 82 percent who answered "yes" were then asked if they were worried about the population increase; 29 percent answered "yes," 65 percent were not worried, and 6 percent did not know. Following that, the public was asked if anything should be done to control the increase in population, and it answered as shown in Table II–18.

Table II–18. Control of Population Growth, 1965 (*Look*)

Statement	Agreement Percentage
Use birth-control methods, including pills.	33%
Educate and advise as to birth control.	25
Miscellaneous (sterilization, war abortions, government aid, and more work and other ways to keep people busy).	14
Do nothing; it's up to the individual.	22
Don't know / No answer	19
Total	113%*

*Some persons gave more than one answer.

The "mood" about population in 1965, as gleaned from these items, was one of general awareness; but the awareness was not accompanied by widespread apprehension. The measures advocated for controlling population that had the most support did not involve coercion but depended upon education and voluntary adoption of birth control.

The *Look* survey was made before the publication of *The Population Bomb* and before Zero Population Growth became a significant social movement. Some glimmer that the public may be more worried or more ready to adopt sterner techniques for controlling population growth can be read from their responses to an item that was included on a national poll that Gallup conducted for the National Wildlife Federation in 1969. One of the items on that poll concerned attitudes toward population limitation:

It has been said that it will, at some time, be necessary to limit the human population (number of people) if our present living standards are to be maintained. Do you think this will be necessary or not (AIPO)?

Yes	*No*	*Don't Know*
44%	43%	13%

While the term "necessary" does not have any specific behavioral referent, it suggests stronger measures than education and advice.

The public's attitudes toward the dissemination and use of the "pill," which is the most widely used contraceptive in the United States, are shown in their responses to the items in Table II–19. In 1970, the same Item 2 appeared on another national survey, and this

Table II–19.   Situations Applicable to Birth Control, 1965
(*Look* and AIPO)

Item	*Response*	
1. What situations can you think of where you would approve of the use of birth-control methods, such as contraceptive pills (*Look*)?	Where poor economic conditions exist	30%
	Where family is already large or large enough	18
	Where mental or physical health is involved	17
	In overpopulated areas	7
	Where individuals are on relief or receiving other government help (welfare, aid to dependent children, and so on)	6
	General approval *or* For people who want it	8
	Other	12
	None; leave it up to the individual	18
	Total	116%*
2. Do you think birth-control pills should be made available free to all women on relief of child-bearing age (AIPO)?	Yes	62%
	No	28
	No opinion	10

*Some persons gave more than one answer.

time the proportion who answered "yes" dropped to 53 percent, 35 percent said "no," and 10 percent had no opinion (AIPO). The drop from 62 to 53 percent was more likely caused by the negative publicity that the pill received from various medical authorities concerning its dangerous side effects than by a change of opinion concerning the rightness or wrongness of its free distribution to a particular class of women. Evidence for this interpretation may be seen in the pattern of responses to the three items that comprise Table II-20. These responses indicate that the public has been

Table II-20. Attitude on Pill after Knowledge of Side Effects, 1967-1970 (AIPO)

Item	Year	Yes	No	No Opinion
1. Do you think these pills are effective—that is, do they work or not?	1967 1970	63% 61	9% 7	28% 32
2. Would you recommend them to a woman who does not want more children?	1967 1970	54% 38	31% 44	15% 18
3. Do you think these pills can be used safely—that is, without danger to a person's health?	1967 1970	43% 23	26% 43	31% 34

changing its mind about the pill. Between 1967 and 1970 there was a considerable drop in the proportion of people who "believed in" the pill; that is, who were not fearful of it or who were willing to recommend it. The reason for the shift is clearly not because they no longer believed in its effectiveness as a means for limiting births—as witness the lack of change in response to Item 1. The negative and widespread publicity that the pill received was, I think, the most likely explanation for the shift in opinion.

Related to the issue of population growth and the desirability of its control are laws affecting abortion and sterilization. In 1966, questions on both these issues were included in national polls. The items pertaining to abortion are shown in Table II-21. The responses indicate that the public supported some loosening of the laws restricting abortions, especially when the mother's health was in danger. There was little support, however (18 percent), for legiti-

Table II-21.   Abortion, 1966 (AIPO)

Item	Should	Should Not	No Opinion
1. Do you think abortion opera- tions should or should not be legal when *the health of* *the mother* is in danger?	77%	16%	7%
2. Do you think abortion operations should or should not be legal when the child may be born deformed?	54	32	14
3. Do you think abortion operations should or should not be legal when the family does not have enough money to support another child?	18	72	10

mizing induced abortions for financial reasons. But a significant shift in attitudes on this matter occurred after 1966.

In November 1969, the public was asked whether it favored a law that would permit a woman to go to a doctor to end a pregnancy at any time during the first three months (AIPO). In response, 40 percent said they favored such a law, 50 percent opposed, and 10 percent had no opinion. At the time of writing, the state of New York has passed a law legalizing abortions for women who are less than 26 weeks into their pregnancy and making the decision a medical one to be determined by the physician and his patient. Other states now have bills in their legislatures proposing much the same procedure.

Sterilization is a more drastic measure, in that it has longer-term consequences than does the act of inducing an abortion. Yet, it apparently does not carry as much of a moral stigma—as witness the responses to the items in Table II-22. The public appears to favor sterilization[17] more than abortions as a method of controlling population expansion—as witness their responses to Items 2 and 3 in Table II-22, compared to Items 2 and 3 in the survey on abortions (Table II-21).

The controversy over the relationship between the rate of

---

[17] In 1970, the public was asked whether it approved or disapproved of the idea of voluntary male sterilization; 53 percent said they approved (AIPO).

Table II-22.   Sterilization, 1966 (AIPO)

Item	Approve	Disapprove	No Opinion
1. Do you approve or dis-approve of sterilization operations in cases where the health of a mother would be endangered by having additional children?	78%	13%	9%
2. Do you approve or dis-approve of sterilization operations on persons who have mental or physical afflictions and who ask to be sterilized?	76	15	9
3. Do you approve or dis-approve of sterilization operations on women who have more children than they can provide for properly and ask to be sterilized?	64	24	12

population growth and natural resources and the implications of that relationship for health and prosperity still rages. There are those in Zero Population Growth who advocate stringent and coercive measures for limiting family size even in the United States, where the immediate population problem is nowhere as urgent as India's, for example. Others, such as Colin Clark (1967), Simon Kuznets (1960), and Ansley Coale (1968) believe that the present rate of population growth in the United States will not lead to the disastrous consequences proclaimed by advocates of zero population growth. Food and other natural resources will not disappear or be "eaten up" by the increasing number of people. Indeed, the economy will prosper as other developed economies have prospered during periods of population expansion in earlier times.

Public opinion tapped in 1965 showed that 29 percent were worried about population growth. Four years later, in 1969, 44 percent said that they thought it would be "necessary to limit population if our present living standards are to be maintained" (*Look*, "The Mood of America 1965: A National Study"). While the two questions are not exactly comparable, the responses to both suggest a trend in the direction of greater concern. Willingness to place one's faith in the pill had, however, declined considerably by 1970.

Public responses on the abortion and sterilization issues may or may not be further proof of the public's concern over population. A position that favors legalizing abortions could be independent of concern about population and stem only from the desire to widen the scope for individual choice about one's destiny.

Two final comments about the public's response to the population issue. Between 1936 and 1971 the following item appeared on at least eleven national surveys:

> The ideal number of children in a family is four or more (AIPO).

Table II-23.   Ideal Number of Children Four or More, 1936-1971 (AIPO)

Year	Agreement Percentage
1936	34%
1941	41
1945	49
1947	47
1953	41
1957	38
1960	45
1963	42
1966	35
1967	40
1971	23

As the responses in Table II-23 show, in no previous year, not even during the depression, did the percent who agreed with the statement drop lower than that reported in 1971.

The second comment is a quotation from a report issued in September 1971 by the Washington Center for Metropolitan Studies:

> the number of pre-school children in the United States declined sharply in the 1960s making zero population growth within this century a distinct possibility.

The report went on to say that the decline in children under 5 years of age from more than 20 million in 1960 to about 17 million in 1970 was by far the largest since recordkeeping began in 1850.

SUGGESTED READINGS

Bernstein, B. J., and A. J. Matusow. *The Truman Administration.* New York, 1966.

Bogue, Donald. *Principles of Demography.* New York, 1961.

Burns, James MacGregor. *Roosevelt: The Lion and the Fox.* New York, 1956.

Clark, Colin. *Population Growth and Land Use.* New York, 1967.

Coale, Ansley J. "Should the United States Start a Campaign for Fewer Births?" *Population Index,* 34 (October–December, 1968), 467–474.

Dewey, John. *The Public and Its Problem.* New York, 1927.

Douglas, Paul. *Social Security in the United States.* New York, 1936.

Ehrlich, Paul. *The Population Bomb.* New York, 1968.

Freidal, Frank. *Franklin D. Roosevelt.* New York, 1952.

Key, V. O. *Public Opinion and American Democracy.* New York, 1961.

Kuznets, Simon. "Population Change and Aggregate Output." In *Demographic and Economic Change in Developed Countries.* Princeton, 1960.

Landsberg, Hans H., *et al. Resources in America's Future.* Baltimore, 1963.

Lindleys, Ernest K. *The Roosevelt Revolution.* New York, 1933.

President's Committee on Civil Rights. *To Secure These Rights.* Washington, D.C., 1947, reprinted 1967.

Rainwater, Lee. *And the Poor Get Children.* Chicago, 1960.

Tocqueville, Alexis de. *Democracy in America.* New York, 1947.

Truman, David B. *The Government Process.* New York, 1951.

Williams, Robin. *American Society.* New York, 1952.

Wise, A. *Rich Schools, Poor Schools: The Promises of Equal Educational Opportunity.* Chicago, 1968.

III
NEGROES AND CIVIL RIGHTS

This chapter describes trends in the opinions of white Americans toward black Americans and civil rights from the late 1930's to the middle 1960's. The next chapter focuses on opinions about Jews in the same time period. In both chapters we try to answer these questions: Have there been significant shifts in opinion over time? If there have, what direction have the shifts taken, and what implications do those changes have for the future?[1]

It was not until the United States was an active participant in the war against Nazism and fascism in the 1940's that questions concerning the lack of congruence between the observed and the ideal status of Negroes in American society were widely discussed in the mass media and by national polling agencies. For example, the beginning of the 1940's was the first time that items appeared on national polls probing the discrepancy between the constitutional rights of Negroes and their observed treatment and the legitimacy of the policy of segregation.

Gunnar Myrdal's *An American Dilemma,* the monumental study of race relations in the United States that focused on the inconsistencies between American values and the established treatment of Negroes, was published in 1944. Since the early 1940's, the topics of racism in American society, white attitudes toward Negroes, Negroes' responses to discrimination and prejudice, and the

---

[1]For an excellent review of this topic, see Schwartz (1966), Hyman and Sheatsley (1956), and Sheatsley (1966).

activities of the judicial, legislative and executive branches of the federal government have been extensively studied and reported.

Harry Truman was the first President since the Civil War to make civil rights an important national issue.[2] On February 2, 1948, he sent a special message to the Congress in which he recommended that the Congress enact legislation directed toward:

1. Establishing a permanent Commission on Civil Rights, a Joint Congressional Committee on Civil Rights, and a Civil Rights Division in the Department of Justice.
2. Strengthening existing civil-rights statutes.
3. Providing federal protection against lynching.
4. Protecting more adequately the right to vote.
5. Establishing a Fair Employment Practices Commission to prevent unfair discrimination in employment.
6. Prohibiting discrimination in interstate transportation facilities.
7. Providing home-rule and suffrage in Presidential elections for the residents of the District of Columbia.

In elaborating these points, Truman talked specifically about providing stronger statutory protection of the right to vote. Such protection was in fact not provided by the Congress until 1964, with the passage of the Civil Rights Act. The prohibition against discrimination in interstate commerce came about as an aftermath of the Supreme Court decision on school desegregation in 1954. Home rule and suffrage for the residents of the District of Columbia were also finally enacted but not during Truman's administration.

INTELLIGENCE ISSUE AND SCHOOL DESEGREGATION

The item that evoked the greatest shift in white reponses over the decades involved concerned the relative intelligence of Negroes as compared to whites. June 1942 was the first time a national survey asked this question:

[2]Truman's initial concerns about civil rights may have been inspired, at least in part, by his fear that Henry Wallace, who had recently announced his candidacy for the Presidency on the Progressive Party ticket, would attract many of the "liberal" votes that had traditionally (that is, since 1932) voted Democrat.

In general, do you think Negroes are as intelligent as white people; that is, can they learn just as well if they are given the same education (and training) (NORC)?

Yes	No	Don't Know
42%	48%	10%

The last tine that item appeared on a national survey was 21 years later, in 1963. At that time, 76 percent answered "yes." The same item appeared on national surveys at least four other times over the 21-year period, with results as shown in Graph III·1. Unfortunately, there is a gap of ten years during a period when some important institutional changes were occurring on this problem (between 1946 and 1956), which makes it difficult to trace the rate of opinion change on this specific issue. We note that in the four years between 1942 and 1946 (that is, during much of World War II), there was an increase of 11 percent. If we assume that opinions changed at about the same rate for the following decade, we would

III-1. Percent Saying Negroes Are As Intelligent As Whites, 1942-1963 (NORC)

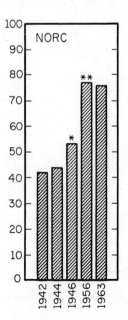

arrive at a figure close to the 77 percent that is reported for 1956. It is clear, however, from the percentages shown that the attitudes of white Americans shifted noticeably in the direction of greater acceptance of an inherent-equality doctrine.

This item has not appeared on a national survey since 1969, when the research by Arthur Jensen was reported—initially in the *Harvard Educational Review* and then in *Newsweek*. Professor Jensen, an educational psychologist at the University of California at Berkeley, claimed that there is a genetic basis for intelligence, that there are biological differences between Negroes and whites affecting native intelligence, and that these differences cannot be ignored in planning curricula and establishing educational policy. Whether Jensen's views have influenced popular opinion so as to alter the direction of the trend toward belief in inherent equality would be worth examining at a later date.

The question that we address ourselves to at the moment is: How did the changes in attitudes as manifested by the responses reported in Graph III–1 influence public attitudes in other spheres, especially in the controversy over integrated versus segregated schools?

On the issue of school desegregation, it is possible to trace changes in white attitudes both to the principle of integration and to the degree of acceptance of change in behavior that followed from the Court's decision. The following item, which was included on at least five national surveys between 1942 and 1965, goes to the matter of principle. The distribution of responses indicates a consistent and steady increase in the percentage of respondents who said they approved of whites and Negroes going to the same school.

Do you think white students and Negro students should go to the same schools or to separate schools (NORC)?

1942	1956	1963	1964[3]	1965
30%	49%	62%	63%	67%

A few weeks after the Supreme Court ruled on the illegality of segregated public-school systems, the public was asked whether it approved or disapproved of the Court's decision. The data in Graph III–2 show that in 1954, the public response was split: 54 percent

[3] In 1964, when a national sample of Negroes was asked this question, 92 percent answered "the same school."

III-2. Percent Approving of School-Desegregation Decision, 1954–1961 (AIPO)

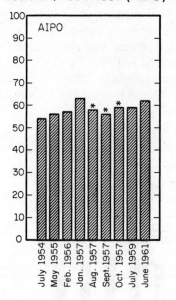

indicated approval; 41 percent disapproval, and 5 percent said they had no opinion. Between 1954 and 1961, the distribution of responses to this item remained relatively stable. The proportion who indicated approval fluctuated between 54 and 62 percent.[4] The percentages in Graph III-2 also show that support for the Court's decision matched closely the percentages who supported integrated schools during those same years.

It is ironic that in 1956, when 77 percent of those polled answered that they believed Negroes were as intelligent as white

[4] In 1970, a Harris survey reported that 61 percent said *de jure* school segregation—separate but equal schools under the law—was wrong, 18 percent disagreed (did not think it wrong), and 21 percent had no opinion. Comparing the distribution of responses in 1970 to that shown for 1961 in Graph III-2, we note that the differences are in the "disapprove" (or support for desegregation) and "no opinion" columns. The percent who approved (or who thought *de jure* segregation was wrong) show no noticeable increase for the past decade and a half.

people, only 49 percent (comparing responses to the two items during the same period, 1956) approved of Negro children attending the same schools as white children (NORC). When the item on the Supreme Court's decision on school desegregation was asked only of *southern* whites, the percent who approved did not go above 20 at any time between 1954 and 1961 (AIPO).[5]

Responses to the following item indicate even more dramatically the public's lack of support for the implications of the Court's decision on school desegregation:

> Would you object to having your children attend a school where the *majority* of pupils are Negroes (AIPO)?

III-3.   **Percent Opposed to Child in School Where Majority Is Negro, 1954-1970 (AIPO)**

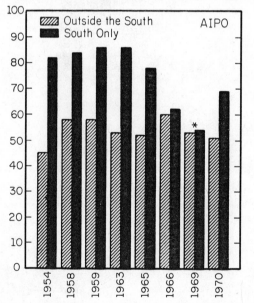

[5] But in the same 1970 Harris survey cited above, 48 percent of the people who lived in the South said they believed *de jure* school segregation was wrong. Thus the segment of the population who shifted their opinion significantly in the direction of greater acceptance were persons living in the area of the country most directly affected by the Court's decision.

Graph III-3 shows that in the sixteen years, from the time of the initial announcement of the doctrine until the period when Northerners, especially those living in large urban centers, realized that *de facto* segregation was as much a target of the Court's subsequent decisions as were the official policies of the southern states, the public became *less* rather than more supportive of the doctrine of "integration with all deliberate speed." By 1966, the trends were such that there was practically no difference in responses between the North and the South. But by 1970, when the prospect that busing in the South would become more widespread and involve much greater numbers of children, there was again a divergence of opinion, with southern responses more anti-integration than northern.

When the same item was asked, but instead of a "majority" of Negro pupils the proportion was "half," the percent who objected dropped from 39 in 1954 to 24 in 1970 in the North and from 81 to 43 in the South. When the number of Negro children in question was "a few," the percent in the North dropped from 13 to 6 and in the South from 72 to 16 for the same time period (AIPO).

Closely related to the issue of how quickly and how extensively a local school is to be integrated is the problem of how it is to be done. Thus far, the busing of children across school districts is the technique used most often. It is a technique, that even in 1970, more than a decade and a half since the Supreme Court's initial decision on the topic, is strongly opposed by more than 75 percent of those questioned. In March 1970, 81 percent said they opposed "the busing of Negro and white school children from one school district to another" (AIPO); and eight months later, in reviewing the results of local referendums on this issue, the *Gallup Opinion Index* reported that 78 percent had indicated their opposition to "busing school children in order to achieve a better racial balance" (AIPO).

The responses to these items—attitudes toward the integration decision, feelings about having one's children attend a school with a majority of Negro children, and the busing of children across school districts—point up a basic dilemma in American society. In principle, almost two-thirds of the respondents said that they supported integration. But the closer to home and the more realistic the implications of school integration became, the less willing were white Americans to go along, especially those who said they favored integration in principle.

TRANSPORTATION, HOUSING AND EMPLOYMENT

In other areas involving public facilities such as transportation, housing, and employment opportunities, there have been dramatic shifts in attitudes that indicate continued and widespread support for civil-rights legislation. Beginning in 1942 and periodically over the next two decades, when asked whether there should be separate sections for Negroes in streetcars and buses, the public exhibited an increase in a pro-civil-rights direction of almost 100 percent from 44 to 79 percent between 1942 and 1963, as shown in Graph III-4.

III-4.   **Percent Disapproving of Separate Sections in Buses, 1942-1963 (AIPO and NORC)**

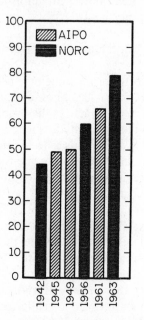

On the housing issue, when asked whether it would make any difference to them if a Negro with just as much income and education moved into their block, the public responded consistently in a direction that supported civil rights. In October 1966 on Graph III-5 we note a sharp drop (even though the wording of the question was unchanged between 1965 and 1966): only 49 percent said they

III-5. **Percent Saying It Would Make No Difference If Negro Moved into Their Block, 1942–1966 (NORC and HAR)**

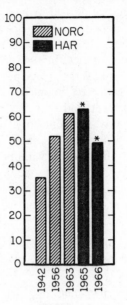

did not object to having a Negro living next door. This figure is even lower than that shown for 1956. The acceptance of Negro neighbors is obviously a more sensitive index of social equality than is agreement that Negroes ought to be able to share the same section of a train or bus. In the items that concerned school desegregation, many more respondents, especially those living in the North, favored desegregation until it involved their own children, especially if their children were likely to have more than minimal exposure to Negroes. A similar pattern obtained with respect to housing. The drop in white respondents who were willing to reduce "social distance" may have been a reaction to the civil disturbances that occurred during 1964 and 1965 in which Negroes living in northern urban districts participated.

What the data presented thus far have shown was a willingness to verbalize support for civil rights in the abstract and insofar as they affected impersonal matters. But greater intimacy, as manifested by neighborhood integration and *de facto* school integration, was still not desired or even acceptable to a majority of white Americans in the North or South.

Following the end of World War II, there was a concerted effort by President Truman, civil-rights organizations, and liberal members of the Congress to gain enactment of a law guaranteeing fair employment opportunities. In 1945, 43 percent favored a law which would require employers to hire a person if he qualified for the job, regardless of his race or color (AIPO). From 1944 to 1946, between 42 and 47 percent said that they thought Negroes should have as good a chance as white people to get any kind of job (NORC).

When asked how far the federal government should go in requiring employers to hire people without regard to race, religion, color, or nationality, only about one-third of the respondents favored direct and significant federal intervention, as indicated by Table III-1. The largest category supported no federal action at all.

Table III-1.   Federal Intervention to Require Nondiscriminatory Hiring, 1948-1950 (AIPO)

Year	All the Way	None of the Way	Depends on Type of Work	Leave to State Government	No Opinion
1948	32%	45%	7%	2%	14%
1949	34	45	5	2	14
1950	34	41	14	*	11

*In 1950, this choice was not given.

In the early 1950's, the public was asked to choose between state and federal intervention. About the same proportion who had answered "None of the Way" in Table III-1 indicated that they favored having each state decide for itself. (Presumably, that meant that each state could decide not to act at all.) In 1952 and 1953, when asked whether there should be a national law requiring employers to hire people without regard to color or race, or whether the issue should be left to each state to decide for itself, about the same proportion, (32 percent) who had answered "All the Way" on Table III-1 favored a national law, and about the same proportion (44-47 percent) who said "None of the Way" advocated "leaving it up to the states" (AIPO). In reviewing the level of responses to the series of items concerning federal intervention in providing more equal employment opportunities for Negroes, we note that no more than 43 percent favored such action between 1944 and 1953.

A decade later, which by then was the third year of the Kennedy administration, each of these items appeared again on national polls. The changes in public opinion as represented by the level of responses to these same items are dramatic. For example, when asked in 1963 whether Negroes should have as good a chance as white people to get any kind of job, 82 percent answered "yes" (HAR). This figure is an increase of almost 50 percent since 1944 and 1946. When asked about a national law requiring employers to hire people without regard to color or race, 86 percent said they favored such a national law (NORC). This is an increase of over 100 percent since 1950. By the 1960's, on the matter of employment opportunities, the trend was clearly and strongly in favor of civil rights for Negroes.

The direction and level of responses to these items are consistent with the responses to items involving housing, public transportation, and education.[6] On each of these issues, the more distant or abstract the problem, the greater the shift of opinion toward a pro-civil-rights position. The provisions in the Civil Rights Act of 1964 include many of the topics about which public opinion had shifted from the 1940's and 1950's to the middle 1960's. The frustrations that the Truman administration experienced in gaining passage of a civil-rights law bore fruit a decade and a half later in the Kennedy–Johnson era.

Table III-2, based on responses to a national survey conducted in December 1963, is a good summary of white attitudes as of that date. The range of prointegration responses between Items 1 and 8 is consistent with the impressions gained from the item-by-item analyses, which are that a high proportion of white Americans support impersonal and institutionalized expressions of tolerance but that more intimate contacts, such as those manifested by gestures of friendship or neighborliness, invitations to one's home, or marriage are still resisted or disapproved of by most whites.

---

[6] In the summer of 1964, the Congress passed the Civil Rights Act that outlawed racial discrimination in hiring and firing wherever interstate commerce was involved, forbade the use of federal grants-in-aid in state programs that were racially discriminatory, outlawed racial discrimination in public accommodation, and provided federal grants for job-retraining programs and vocational education.

Table III-2.   Guttman Scale of Prointegration Sentiment, 1963

Item	Prointegration Percentage
1. Do you think Negroes should have as good a chance as white people to get any kind of job, or do you think white people should have the first chance at any kind of job?	82%
2. Generally speaking, do you think there should be separate sections for Negroes in streetcars and buses?	77
3. Do you think Negroes should have the right to use the same parks, restaurants, and hotels as white people?	71
4. Do you think white students and Negro students should go to the same schools or to separate schools?	63
5. How strongly would you object if a member of your family wanted to bring a Negro friend home to dinner?	49
6. White people have a right to keep Negroes out of their neighborhoods if they want to, and Negroes should respect that right.	44
7. Do you think there should be laws against marriages between Negroes and whites?	36
8. Negroes shouldn't push themselves where they're not wanted.	27

Adapted from Paul B. Sheatsley, "White Attitudes Toward the Negro," *Daedalus*, 95 (Winter 1966), 217–237, at p. 224. Reprinted by permission of *Daedalus*, Journal of the American Academy of Arts and Sciences, Boston, Mass. Winter 1966, *The Negro American—2*. To quote Sheatsley: "The properties of a Guttman scale are such that if a person rejects one item on the scale, the chances are at least nine in ten that he will reject all items below it. Thus, those who reject the top item—equal job opportunities for Negroes— are highly unlikely to endorse any of the other items on the scale and may be considered extreme segregationists. At the other end of the scale, the 27 percent who disagree with the proposition that 'Negroes shouldn't push themselves where they're not wanted' are extremely likely to take a prointegration position on all seven of the other items."

DEMONSTRATIONS IN THE 1960's

Many observers of the national scene have described the changes in American society from the silent, stable 1950's to the riot-ridden 1960's as near-revolutionary in their pervasiveness and intensity. In the area of civil rights especially, the 1960's was a period of turbulence and social change. Sheatsley (1966, p. 237) quotes a Gallup release in October 1963 as follows:

> the question of race relations has been consistently cited by Americans as the most important problem facing the United States, "except when it has been temporarily displaced by some international crisis such as Vietnam."

In this section, we examine, and where possible compare, responses of white and black citizens to the demonstrations, marches, riots, looting, and other activities that marked this new era in civil rights.

In 1961 the American public was asked:

> Do you feel demonstrations of Negroes have helped more or hurt more the advancement of Negro rights (AIPO and HAR)?

This item appeared in more or less the same form at least once a year from 1961 through 1967 with the results shown in Graph III-6. The data show a rather consistent trend against support for demonstrations by Negroes on the part of the white community on the grounds that the demonstrations were "hurting more than helping" the Negroes' chances for full social and political equality.[7]

In his study of Negro attitudes "toward their own situation, the whites, the community and the civil rights movement," Gary Marx (1967, p. 15) reported the responses of Negro respondents in 1964 to this parallel item:[8]

> Would you say about the civil-rights demonstrations over the last few years that they have helped Negroes a great deal, helped a little, hurt a little, or a great deal?

About 56 percent answered "helped a great deal," and an additional 30 percent said "helped a little." In the same year, looking at the results in Graph III-6, we note that 21 percent of the white respon-

[7]Nevertheless, when asked in the summer of 1964. "Do people have a *right* to demonstrate on behalf of civil rights?" 61 percent answered "yes."

[8]Marx's sample consisted of Negroes who lived in metropolitan areas outside the South, plus a special sample of Negroes who lived in New York City, Chicago, Atlanta, and Birmingham.

III-6. Percent Saying Demonstrations Hurt Negro Rights, 1961-1967 (AIPO and HAR)

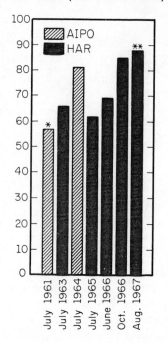

dents believed that demonstrations helped more than hurt the Negroes. The differences between white and Negro opinion on what had become the strategy of the 1960's for calling attention to the situation of Negroes in the United States and for bringing about concrete improvements in their status are dramatically demonstrated by the disparity of responses to this item. The Negro respondents were almost unanimous in their belief that demonstrations helped Negroes, while only 10 percent of the whites during the same period shared that conviction. The item was asked of both the Negroes and whites in the fall of 1964, after the demonstrations and riots of the previous summer.

In the summer of 1961, the white community was asked its opinion about the "freedom rides." The question read:

Do you approve or disapprove of what the Freedom Riders are doing (AIPO)?

In that period, the main participants in the freedom rides were middle-class young people (mostly college students) from northern and southern universities. But even so 64 percent of whites polled answered that they disapproved of such activities. Two years later, 63 percent said they disapproved of the proposed civil-rights demonstration that was planned to follow the march on Washington.[9] This was the march organized by Bayard Rustin and led by Martin Luther King, Jr., in which some 200,000 persons are said to have participated. The march on Washington, the freedom rides, the lunch-counter sit-ins were all demonstrations organized and led by "responsible," middle-class white and black leaders. We had not yet entered the Black Power era, the Black Panthers were either non-existent or not visible outside the ghetto, and men with the rhetoric of a Bobbie Seale, a Rap Brown, an Eldridge Cleaver, or a Huey Newton were not the organizers or the leaders of these acts of protest. Nevertheless, the white community did not support activities that, in retrospect, appear as relatively mild forays into the white establishment.[10]

During the summers of 1963 and 1964, the white community expressed the reactions shown in Table III-3 to specific activities in the "new" civil-rights campaign.

A classic question that members of the establishment ask about groups, movements, or ideas that try to shake the foundation of their social order is: "What" or "who" are the "unseen" or "hidden" forces behind this movement or these people? Historically, the South applied the label "outside agitators" to anyone who tried to organize support for civil rights or to improve the conditions of the Negroes in the South. Northerners also, especially when the campaign for civil rights took to the streets in the 1960's, tended to see the invisible hand of Communists or radicals directing the disruptive

[9]The item was asked only of the 69 percent who had indicated earlier that they had heard or read about the proposed rally (AIPO).

[10]When white attitudes toward integration were divided into four categories (highly in favor, moderately in favor, moderately opposed, and highly opposed) and respondents in each category were then asked "Do you approve or disapprove of the actions Negroes have taken to obtain civil rights?" only a majority of the whites in the "highly in favor" category expressed approval of these actions. The percentage who disapproved was: Highly in favor, 33%; Moderately in favor, 62% Moderately opposed, 73%; Highly opposed, 89% (NORC).

Table III-3.   White Attitude on Civil-Rights
Activities, 1963-1964 (HAR)

Activity / Item	Disapproval Percentage Nationwide
Summer 1963	
Lie down in front of truck at construction sites to protest hiring discrimination	91%
Sit-in at lunch counters	67
Go to jail to protest discrimination	56
Boycott products whose manufacturers don't hire enough Negroes	55
Summer 1964	
1. This summer white and Negro students are going to Mississippi to organize Negroes to vote. Do you generally approve of this move or disapprove of it?	57
2. Do people approve or disapprove of picketing of political conventions as occurred at the Cow Palace in San Francisco?	76
3. People have different views about the Negro demonstrations. Some people say the Negroes should stop their demonstrations now that they have made their point and even though some of their demands have not been met. Others say they have to continue demonstrating in order to achieve better jobs, better housing, and better schools. With which view do you agree? [Stop demonstrating.]	73

activities of the blacks in Harlem, Detroit, Watts, Newark, and elsewhere.

In the fall of 1965, when asked whether they thought that Communists were involved in the demonstrations over civil rights 78 percent of the white respondents said that Communists were involved "a lot" (51 percent) or "to some extent" (27 per cent) (AIPO).

Consistent with the perception that "radicals," "outsiders," or "troublemakers" organized these protests for their own objectives is the belief that the "sources" or reasons for the trouble did not arise out of injustices within the social system. Responsibility for the trouble over civil rights, therefore, could not be placed at the doorstep of the white community. Responses, in Table III–4, to the following item illustrate the white and black communities' differential perception of "who's responsible."

> What do you think are the two or three main reasons riots have broken out in this country (HAR)?

Table III–4.   Main Reasons for Riots, 1967 (HAR)

Reason	Whites	Negroes
Outside agitation	45%	10%
Prejudice, promises not kept, bad treatment	16	36
Poverty, slums, ghetto conditions	14	28
Lack of jobs, unfair employment	10	29
Negroes too lazy to work for their rights	13	5
Uneducated people who don't know what they're doing	11	9
Total	109%*	117%*

*Some persons gave more than one reason.

Twice as many white respondents placed the blame on outside agitation, Negro laziness, or ignorance as on social and economic conditions within the society or prejudice. Negro respondents, on the other hand, cited social and economic factors and prejudice or discrimination by whites.

Along the same lines, we found that when asked, in 1963, whether they thought "the race revolt" was supported by the rank and file of Negroes, 34 percent of the white respondents said "yes" compared to 91 percent of the Negroes (HAR).[11] Four years later, in the summer of 1967—remembered as a time when the most serious urban race riots in the country occurred, a large majority in both the Negro and white communities believed that most Negroes do *not* support riots. In response to the following item, over 80 percent of both white and Negro respondents agreed that only a minority of the Negro population supported the riots. Specific responses are shown on Table III–5.

[11] Marx (1967, p. 20) reported that in response to the item "To tell the truth I would be afraid to take part in civil rights demonstrations," about 26 percent answered, "yes, that is true." Such responses are consistent with those reported above about rank-and-file support for the race riots.

Do you feel that most Negroes support riots or only a minority (HAR)?

Table III-5.   Extent of Negro Support for Riots, 1967 (HAR)

Respondents	Majority	Minority	Not Sure
Whites	11%	83%	6%
Negroes	10	85	5

The Negro responses to the two items are not inconsistent. The term "race revolt" describes a larger set of behaviors than participation in riots or other forms of violent civil disobedience. Marches, demonstrations, sit-ins, boycotts, pickets, support for black candidates for government offices are other forms the race revolt of the 1960's could and did assume. It is fair to assume that when 91 percent of the Negro respondents said they thought the race revolt was supported by the rank and file of Negroes, it was these kinds of behavior they had in mind—perhaps in addition to rioting. We note also that even though whites and Negroes agreed that only a minority of Negroes supported the riots, they did not agree with the punishment appropriate for such behavior. When asked the questions in Table III-6, in the midst of the August 1967 riots, about two-thirds

Table III-6.   Shooting of Fire-Bomb Throwers and Looters, 1967 (HAR)

Item	Respondents	Should	Should Not	Not Sure
1. Do you feel that people who throw fire bombs in riots should be shot or not?	Whites	68%	22%	10%
	Negroes	47	42	11
2. Do you think looters should be shot or not?	Whites	62%	28%	10%
	Negroes	27	62	11

of the whites favored shooting the fire-bomb throwers and the looters. Negroes differentiated between the two activities more than did whites, judging looting as much less reprehensible. Negroes were also less likely to favor shooting the participants engaged in either activity.

Related to attitudes toward looters and fire-bomb throwers are beliefs about the behavior of white policemen toward Negros. Interestingly enough, the opinions of whites and Negroes on this matter are not far apart. In August 1964, a national survey contained the following item:

> It has been claimed that white policemen often engage in police brutality against Negroes. Do you tend to believe that it is true or not true (HAR)?

And in the survey reported by Marx (1967, p. 36), Negroes were asked:

> How would you say that the police treat Negroes—very well, fairly well, fairly badly, or very badly?

Of the white respondents, 68 percent answered that it was "not true" that white policemen often engaged in brutality against Negroes, and 58 percent of the Negroes said they thought the police treated Negroes "very well" or "fairly well" (HAR).

We conclude with a few comments about the mood of the country concerning civil rights and about white attitudes toward the status of Negroes at the end of a decade that was marked by more internal turbulence and strife than any since the Civil War. Concerning the public's level of apprehension about what was likely to happen next, responses to the following item indicate that the public expected things to get worse before they got better.

> Compared to a year ago, are you personally more worried about race riots, less worried or do you feel about the same as you did then (HAR)?
>
> | | *1966* | *1967* |
> |---|---|---|
> | More worried | 49% | 76% |

As it turned out, there was no "Newark," "Watts," "Detroit," or any other major riot with direct racial overtones during the summers of 1968 and 1969. But as a result of the events of the summer of 1967, a large majority of the American public felt apprehensive and con-concerned about where and when trouble would break out next.

On the larger issue of how whites perceived the general status of the Negro in American society, it is interesting to compare the level of responses to two items: the first was asked on national surveys

Table III-7.   Treatment of Negroes, 1944-1968 (NORC)

Item	Year	Fairly / Same as Whites
1. Do you think most Negroes in the United States are being treated fairly or unfairly?	1944 1946 1956	60% 66 66
2. In your opinion, how well do you think Negroes are treated in this country—the same as whites are, not very well, or badly?	1967 1968	72% 70

in the 1940's and 1950's; the second, in 1967 and 1968. The questions and the responses are shown in Table III-7. Most white people believe today, as they did almost a quarter of a century earlier, that Negroes are treated fairly. One might interpret this response by claiming that to think otherwise would arouse too much guilt within the respondent, and would have to go hand in hand with a recognition that important and extensive changes were needed in American society. But probably the explanation is simpler. The widely held belief that Negroes are treated fairly is not a defensive reaction or an opinion that is held out of an unwillingness to accept the consequences of believing differently. Rather it is probably the way most white Americans see it.[12] For example, they were asked the following question in 1968:

> Who is more to blame for the present conditions in which Negroes find themselves—white people or Negroes themselves (AIPO)?

More than twice as many answered "Negroes": Whites, 22%; Negroes, 58%; No opinion, 20%. These responses are consistent with the ones shown above, in that most people recognize that the conditions under which most Negroes live are not as good as those under which most whites live. But most of them do not believe that the whites are to blame. They do not blame themselves for the poorer living conditions, slower occupational advancement, or fewer years

[12]This view is not unrelated to opinions expressed by Negro respondents when asked in 1964: "Do you think that in general things are getting better or getting worse for Negroes in this country?" In response, 80 percent answered "better."

of schooling of most Negroes. It also follows that when asked about the conclusion of the President's Commission on Civil Disorders (1968) claiming that "our nation is moving toward two societies, one black, one white—separate and unequal," most whites did not agree: Agree, 32%; Disagree, 52%; No opinion, 16% (AIPO).

Most white Americans do not accept the conclusion that the United States is a racist society, that blacks are treated unfairly, and that separateness and inequality in social matters are basic dimensions of American life. Instead, they focus on the institutional changes that have occurred in such areas as public transportation, housing, education, and employment opportunities. Arguing on the basis of such indices that Negroes have been integrated into American society, they contend that the riots, demonstrations, and protests are not justified. Most whites do not believe that Negroes are treated unfairly. In the absence of that feeling, there is not much basis for optimism that in the forseeable future blacks will become first-class citizens in American society in contexts and behavior that go beyond "formal" equality and institutionalized integration.

SUGGESTED READINGS

Brink, William, and Lewis Harris. *Black and White: A Study of U.S. Racial Attitudes Today.* New York, 1967.

Broom, Leonard, and Norval Glenn. *Transformation of the Negro American.* New York, 1965.

Carmichael, Stokely, and Charles V. Hamilton. *Black Power: The Politics of Liberation in America.* New York, 1967.

Crain, Robert L. *The Politics of School Desegregation: Comparative Case Studies of Community Structure and Policy Making.* Chicago, 1967.

Glenn, Norval, and Charles Bonjean, eds. *Blacks in the United States.* San Francisco, 1969.

Hyman, Herbert H., and Paul B. Sheatsley. "Attitudes toward Desegregation." *Scientific American,* 195 (December 1956), 35–39.

Hyman, Herbert H., and Paul B. Sheatsley. "Attitudes toward Desegregation—Seven Years Later." *Scientific American,* 211 (July 1964), 16–23.

Jensen, Arthur R. "How Much Can We Boost IQ and Scholastic Achievement?" *Harvard Educational Review,* 39, No. 1 (1969), 1–123. *Newsweek,* March 31, 1969, and June 2, 1969.

Kalven, Harry, Jr. *The Negro and the First Amendment.* Columbus, 1965.

Marx, Gary. *Protest and Prejudice.* New York, 1967.

Myrdal, Gunnar, *et al. An American Dilemma.* New York, 1944.

Parsons, Talcott, and Kenneth Clark, eds. *The Negro American.* Boston, 1966.

Report of the National Advisory Commission on Civil Disorders. New York, 1968.

Schwartz, Mildred A. *Trends in White Attitudes toward Negroes.* Chicago, 1966.

Silberman, Charles. *Crisis in Black and White.* New York, 1964.

Simpson, George, and Milton Yinger. *Racial and Cultural Minorities: An Analysis of Prejudice and Discrimination.* 3rd ed.; New York, 1965.

Tumin, Melvin. *Desegregation: Resistance and Readiness.* Princeton, 1958.

United States Commission on Civil Rights. *Racial Isolation in the Public Schools.* Washington, D.C., 1967.

Waskow, Arthur I. *From Race Riot to Sit In.* New York, 1966.

Williams, Robin. *The Reduction of Intergroup Tensions: A Survey of Research on Problems of Ethnic, Racial and Religious Group Relations.* Bulletin 57; New York, 1947.

Williams, Robin, Jr., *et al. Strangers Next Door: Ethnic Relations in American Communities.* Englewood Cliffs, N.J., 1964.

IV
JEWS IN AMERICA
AND ABROAD

Between 1966 and the present, two major studies of anti-Semitism in the United States were commissioned by Jewish agencies and carried out by reputable social scientists. The first, *Jews in the Mind of America* by Charles H. Stember and his associates, appeared in 1966 and was sponsored by the American Jewish Committee. The second, *The Tenacity of Prejudice: Anti-Semitism in Contemporary America* by Gertrude J. Selznick and Stephen Steinberg, was published in 1969. The Selznick-Steinberg volume is the fourth in a series entitled "Patterns of American Prejudice," which is part of the University of California's five-year study of anti-Semitism sponsored by the Anti-Defamation League of B'nai Brith. Another volume in that series, *Protest and Prejudice* by Gary Marx, published in 1967, deals in part with Negro attitudes toward Jews and considers the phenomenon of Negro anti-Semitism.

The first section of the Stember volume (1966, p. 31) analyzes national poll data from 1937 to 1962 concerning American attitudes toward Jews:

> . . . these surveys dealt with beliefs and sentiments concerning Jews in a great many contexts, against the constantly shifting background of world events in that tragic quarter-century. Thus, the evidence assembled here constitutes an extended footnote to American and

American-Jewish history, documenting the nature and trend of anti-Semitism during a crucial period.

The second part consists of a series of essays by eminent historians and social scientists on various aspects of anti-Semitism and the Jewish experience in the United States.

The Selznick-Steinberg volume also analyzes survey data about the nature and extent of anti-Semitism in the United States, but in a different way. Instead of analyzing existent poll data for trends over time, the authors designed their own survey and supervised the collection of 1,967 interviews at a specific period in time: three weeks before the 1964 Presidential election. Their study asked three questions (p. xiii):

> How much anti-Semitism is there? Where—among what kinds of people is it most prevalent? And, finally, why are some kinds of people more likely than others to be anti-Semitic?

The striking impression that one is left with after reading both volumes is that while the authors are not in basic disagreement about what the data say, they come away with profoundly different impressions about the implications of their findings and their projections for the future. Stember concludes his volume on an optimistic, positive note (p. 208):

> . . . anti-Semitism in all its forms has massively declined in the United States between the prewar or war years and the early 1960s.

Selznick and Steinberg do not disagree with that observation. But in the first sentence of their concluding chapter, they comment as follows (p. 184):

> Two basic conclusions emerge from this study: anti-Semitism continues at significant levels, and lack of education is the primary factor in its acceptance.

Stember goes on to note (p. 217):

Anti-Jewish prejudice obviously is not yet a thing of the past, any more than anti-Jewish discrimination is, but both are unmistakably in a state of decline. As we have seen, hostile attitudes toward Jews are finding less widespread support in the 1960s than at any other time since the systematic study of public attitudes began. Actual discriminatory practices also have lessened to a marked degree during that period, so that we probably are safe in asserting that the prejudices and discrimination today are not prevalent enough to reinforce or perpetuate each other significantly, as they formerly did. In both feeling and behavior toward Jews, our society has undergone a profound change within the span of one generation.

But we may confidently state that the current trend toward more and more complete acceptance of the Jew— both individually and in the abstract—appears unlikely to be reversed by anything short of a catastrophic crisis in American society. The longer such a crisis is averted, the more firmly will recognition of Jews as equal and respected fellow citizens become grounded in the mores of the American people.

Selznick and Steinberg conclude (p. 185):

Nevertheless, a resurgence of anti-Semitism cannot be ruled out. This study has presented a large body of evidence pointing to the conclusion that cultural resources for fascism are widespread in American society. The continued existence of anti-Semitic prejudice would not by itself justify such a conclusion. As our data show, the anti-Semitism of most Americans does not go beyond acceptance of anti-Semitic beliefs and support of mild forms of discrimination. Nor is it a foregone conclusion that political reaction in the United States would be accompanied by anti-Semitism. However, simplistic beliefs and authoritarian attitudes, ignorance and disregard of democratic norms, a low threshold of tolerance for social and political diversity, insensitivity to the suffering of others—these are tendencies that characterize large numbers of Americans. Given a crisis situation and political leadership, they constitute a potential threat to the democratic order.

With these two studies and their differing expectations concerning the future as background, we turn to an analysis of the national poll data that describe attitudes toward Jews from the 1930's to the 1960's. The next section reports Negro attitudes toward Jews. Then we briefly consider the public's attitude toward the condition of Jews in Germany in the 1930's and toward accepting refugees. Finally we explore the public's support or lack of support for the founding of a Jewish state in the Middle East after World War II.

ANTI-SEMITISM: PERSISTENCE OR DISAPPEARANCE

An American sociologist writing about anti-Semitism in the United States in the 1960's might have the memory of the Jewish community in Germany during the period of the Weimar Republic sharply etched in his mind. The similarities between the 600,000 Jews who lived in Germany in the 1920's and the more than 5,000,000 who lived in the United States in the 1960's have been commented upon, nervously, by observers familiar with both periods. Each community, in its time, has been referred to as the modern "Golden Age" of Jewry in the diaspora. In both countries Jews had been accepted and had appeared to be integrated into the national culture. In some spheres, such as the mass media, the entertainment industry, the professions, many Jews were and are recognized as leaders. Intermarriage, which is viewed by some as a measure of integration, was higher in the 1920's in Germany than in other Western countries. Today it is higher in the United States than in other Western societies. Jewish institutions, that is, synagogues and temples, hospitals, schools, and social centers, were and are abundant and flourishing. The over-all socioeconomic status of the Jews (their jobs, income, and education) placed them in Germany and places them in the United States in the most comfortable and successful strata of both societies.

The tragedy that marked the end of the "Golden Age of German Jewry" is familiar to most of us. The question that remains is: How will the Jewish community in the United States fare over the next decade or so? Some observers, among them Norman Podhoretz, editor of *Commentary*, and Seymour Lipset, a sociologist at Harvard, are fearful of the future. Podhoretz sees the need for scapegoats to explain America's first military defeat (in Vietnam) and believes that Jewish leftists and/or intellectuals will be accused of having stabbed the military in the back. Lipset emphasizes the growing anti-Semitism of the New Left arising in part out of a distrust of the state of Israel and a need to identify with underdogs—be they blacks in the United States or Arabs in the Middle East. Others note the growing concern over our domestic economy and are fearful that there will be a major depression for which the Jews will bear a disproportionate share of either the blame or the hardship. They also believe that there are persons who occupy important positions in the major political parties and the government who would not be averse to using latent feelings of anti-Semitism for their own political advantage. Any one of these possibilities, alone or in combination— losing a war, a major depression, anti-Israel sentiment, or political manipulation of latent traditional forms of anti-Semitism—could produce important changes in the public's attitudes toward the Jews.

Prior to the publication of the Stember volume and the funding of the anti-Semitism study at the University of California, interest in anti-Semitism on the part of the major polling agencies had declined steadily from the mid-1930's to the mid-1960's. From 1936 to 1945, 35 items pertaining to anti-Semitism appeared on national polls. In the next decade (1946–1955) the number dropped to 25, and in the last decade, 1956–1965, only 20 items were included.

In 1937, the public was asked whether it thought anti-Semitism was increasing or decreasing in the United States. Respondents fell into four categories of almost equal size: Increasing, 29%; Decreasing, 23%; Remaining the same, 25%; No opinion, 23% (AIPO).

In 1939, the same item was repeated. This time, however, more than twice as many said they thought anti-Semitism was increasing. The distribution of responses in 1939 was: Increasing, 45%; Decreasing, 17%; Remaining the same, 16%; No opinion, 22% (AIPO).

Along the same lines, the public was asked in 1939:

1. Do you believe that in this country hostility toward the Jewish people is growing or not (FOR)?
2. Do you think there is likely to be a widespread campaign against the Jews in this country (AIPO)?
3. Would you support such a campaign (AIPO)?

In response, 33 percent said they thought anti-Semitism was growing, 20 percent said that there was likely to be a widespread campaign against Jews in this country, and 12 percent said they would support such a campaign. That 12 percent represented the hard core of anti-Semitic feeling in the United States in 1939. They were people who said that they would actively participate in campaigns against Jews. Selznick and Steinberg claimed that in 1964 "over a third of Americans" were anti-Semitic, but their instrument measured attitudes and beliefs. The instrument was an eleven-item "Index of Anti-Semitic Belief" (reproduced as Table IV-5 in this chapter). It did not ask what the respondent would be willing to *do* to support their attitudes. Thus, the 12 percent figure should not be interpreted to mean that anti-Semitism had increased threefold between 1939 and 1964. The behavioral measure probably tapped more intense and hardened anti-Semitic beliefs than did the index used in the 1964 study.

THE IMAGE OF THE JEW

We look now at what the American public's image of the Jew in this country was in the 1930's and at how that image changed or did not change between the 1930's and the 1960's.

In 1939, the following item appeared on a national poll, and the responses are shown in Table IV-1.

Which of the following statements most clearly represents your general opinion on the Jewish question (FOR)?

In response, 33 percent expressed opinions that ranged from advocating a policy of "genteel segregation" to supporting a policy of mass exile of all Jews from the United States. About the same proportion favored treating the Jews like any other Americans as advocated segregation or control of activities.

The following question concerning personality or moral characteristics was asked in various forms in 1938, 1940, and then again in 1962. The responses are given in Table IV-2.

Are there any qualities about Jews to which you object? (If yes: What qualities do you object to in Jews?) (OPOR and AIPO).

Table IV–1.   Attitude on Jewish Question, 1939 (FOR)

Statement	Agreement Percentage
1. In the United States the Jews have the same standing as any other people, and they should be treated in all ways exactly as any other American.	39%
2. Jews are in some ways distinct from other Americans, but they make respected and useful citizens so long as they don't try to mingle socially where they are not wanted.	11
3. Jews have some different business methods and, therefore, some measures should be taken to prevent Jews from getting too much power in the business world.	32
4. We should make it a policy to deport Jews from this country as fast as it can be done with humanity.	10
5. Don't know / No answer	8

We note first that between 1938 and 1962, the proportion who said that Jews had qualities to which they objected dropped from 58 and 63 percent to 22 per cent. Some (how much, we do not know) of this

Table IV–2.   Objectionable Qualities of Jews, 1938–1962 (OPOR and AIPO)

Quality	1938 (OPOR)	1940* (OPOR)	1962* (AIPO)
None mentioned	42%	37%	78%
Greed	13	—	—
Dishonesty †	12	32	6
Aggressiveness	9	12	6
Clannishness	7	11	4
Lack of culture	2	10	1
Selfishness	5	4	1
Overbearance	3	—	—
Appearance	—	4	—
Other	8	4	7
Total	101% ‡	114% ‡	103% ‡

*In 1940 and 1962, the question read: "Are there any objectionable qualities which you think Jews generally have to a greater extent than other people?"

†In 1940 and 1962, the quality was Unscrupulousness.

‡Some persons mentioned more than one quality.

Adapted from Charles H. Stember et al., Jews in the Mind of America (New York, 1966), pp. 54, 65.

drop was due simply to the public's greater sophistication. It was less likely, in the decade of the 1960's, that respondents would impute negative qualities to an entire group of people that they did not like than it had been before World War II. One could argue that this perspective would apply to all items that seek assessments of Jews, Negroes, and any other minority group. The answer, I think, is: "Yes, to some extent." But the item shown above is a particularly gross example of the kind of attitude about which the American public has been most sensitized or educated to reject. Therefore, those who answered such an item in the affirmative in the 1960's felt more strongly negative or objected more vehemently to those qualities than did persons who answered in the affirmative twenty-five or thirty years earlier.

In looking over the distribution of responses, we find that three qualities were mentioned most often in the three surveys: dishonesty or unscrupulousness (and perhaps greed should be included in this category), aggressiveness, and clannishness. These are the same characteristics that probably would have been mentioned in Europe in the Middle Ages or in the nineteenth century, and I would guess will be mentioned in the twenty-first century, although probably by an even smaller group than the 22 percent shown for 1962.

On the other hand, one could probably make the same predictions for the positive qualities that are attributed to Jews. During the same time periods, the following item was asked. The responses are shown in Table IV-3.

> Are there any admirable qualities which you think Jews generally have to a greater extent than other people? (If yes: What qualities do you admire in Jews?) (OPOR and AIPO).

Again, the characteristics mentioned remained relatively stable over the twenty-five years: racial or religious loyalty, ability in business or finance, persistence-ambition, intellectual attainments, and loyalty to family. We note also that the proportion of respondents who answered the question about admirable qualities in the affirmative did not decline as sharply in 1962 as did the proportion of respondents who answered in the affirmative to the item on objectionable qualities. Having a "positive" image of an ethnic or racial minority group does not carry as much of a stigma.

**Table IV-3.   Admirable Qualities of Jews, 1938-1962
(OPOR and AIPO)**

Quality	1938 (OPOR)	1940 (OPOR)	1962 (AIPO)
None mentioned	49%	42%	56%
Ability in business or finance	13	19	13
Racial or religious loyalty	12	17	16
Loyalty to wife and family	8	10	4
Intellectual attainments	7	8	5
Persistence, determination, ambition	6	9	7
Thrift, financial independence	5	—	3
Kindness, generosity, charitableness	4	—	4
Other	5	10	2
Total	109%*	115%*	110%*

*Some persons mentioned more than one quality.
Adapted from Charles H. Stember *et al., Jews in the Mind of America* (New York, 1966), pp. 56, 65.

**IV-1. Percent Saying Jews Have Too Much Power,
1938-1964 (NORC)**

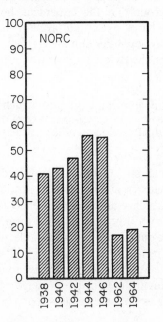

We turn now to some specific items about the image of the Jews or feelings about Jews in the United States, for which there are data extending from the late 1930's to the mid-1960's. The items touch on various questions: occupational and educational opportunities, friendship, and power. Responses to the issue of whether Jews have too much power are shown in Graph IV-1. The figures do not tell us exactly when "the Jewish power threat" receded, except that it was some time after World War II and before 1962. Given the wording of the question, we cannot tell whether respondents believed that Jews possessed less power in the 1960's than they had had previously, or that they had the same or more power than they had had previously, but no more than they *ought* to have.

There are other items, however, about the performance of Jews in various roles, and opinions about the statuses they ought to occupy, that may help interpret the above responses. These items are shown in Table IV-4. Responses to all of these items explain and

Table IV-4.   Performance and Status of Jews, 1938-1962 (NORC)

Item		Response					
1. Do you think Jewish						*1938*	*1962*
businessmen are more	Less					44%	20%
honest or less honest	More					3	2
than other businessmen?	Same					44	78
	No opinion					9	—
2. Do you think colleges						*1938*	*1962*
should limit the number	Yes					26%	4%
of Jews they admit?	No					65	88
	Don't know					9	8
3. If you were an employer			*1940*	*1942*	*1956*	*1962*	
hiring a new employee,	Yes		43%	37%	42%	6%	
would it make any	No		51	57	50	94	
difference to you if he	No opinion		6	6	8	—	
were a Jew?							
4. If you were moving to a		*1940*	*1950*	*1953*	*1956*	*1959*	*1962*
new house and found	Yes*	25%	30%	19%	12%	10%	3%
that your next-door							
neighbor was Jewish,							
would it make any							
difference to you?							

Or Wouldn't like Jewish neighbor at all. In 1940 and 1962, the response categories were "yes" and "no."

support the basis for the optimistic tone of the Stember volume. Both from the trends that were established and from the absolute level of responses, we note sharp reductions in prejudicial impres-

Table IV-5.   Selznick-Steinberg Index of Anti-Semitic Belief, 1969

Statement	Anti-Semitic Percentage
1. Do you think Jews have too much power in the United States?	11%
2. How about the business world—do you think Jews have too much power in the business world?	26
3. Jews are more willing than others to use shady practices to get what they want.	28
4. Jews are more loyal to Israel than to America.	29
5. Jews are (not) just as honest as other businessmen.	30
6. Jews have a lot of irritating faults.	30
7. International banking is pretty much controlled by Jews.	35
8. Jews don't care what happens to anyone but their own kind.	40
9. Jews always like to be at the head of things.	42
10. Jews stick together too much.	52
11. The trouble with Jewish businessmen is that they are so shrewd and tricky that other people don't have a fair chance in competition.	54

Index Score	Percentage	
0	16 ⎫	Least anti-Semitic third, 31%
1	15 ⎭	
2	12 ⎫	
3	10 ⎬	Middle anti-Semitic third, 32%
4	10 ⎭	
5	8 ⎫	
6	6	
7	7	
8	6 ⎬	Most anti-Semitic third, 37%
9	5	
10	3	
11	2 ⎭	

N = 1,913
Average score = 3.75

Adapted from Gertrude J. Selznick and Stephen Steinberg, *The Tenacity of Prejudice: Anti-Semitism in Contemporary America* (New York, 1969), pp. 22–24, 26.

sions to levels that include less than 20 percent of the population.

We indicated earlier that Selznick and Steinberg do not share Stember's optimism about the future. Without attempting to reproduce all of the data they compiled and upon which they then based their conclusions, we report in Table IV-5 the scores and the responses to each item on their "Index of Anti-Semitic Belief," which was the major instrument in their study. The distribution of responses on the index is shown at the bottom of Table IV-5. Those in the least anti-Semitic third accepted one or none of the beliefs, those in the middle third accepted between two and four anti-Semitic beliefs, and those in the most anti-Semitic third accepted between five and eleven beliefs. The authors comment about this distribution as follows:

> The most anti-Semitic third of the sample accept at least
> five of the eleven beliefs in the Index. It is significant that
> to locate the most anti-Semitic third one has to dip as
> low as five on the Index. Had a survey been conducted
> twenty years ago using the same Index, the most anti-
> Semitic third might well have accepted as many as eight
> beliefs. This does not mean that the most anti-Semitic
> third in our sample is not really anti-Semitic. With but
> one exception, every belief in the Index was accepted by
> a majority of the most anti-Semitic third. If the beliefs in
> the Index were put to a vote among this group all but one
> would pass. If the population as a whole were as anti-
> Semitic as the most anti-Semitic third, Americans would
> be very anti-Semitic indeed.

The data to support this last point, about all but one of the items being accepted by persons in the most anti-Semitic third, are reproduced in Table IV-6. It is these findings that provide much of the basis for concern and that leave the analyst with a more somber and less sanguine feeling about the future of the Jewish community and about the pervasiveness of anti-Semitism in American society. Results such as those reproduced above are absent in the data that Stember culled from the national polls conducted between 1937 and 1962. In noting these responses, we reiterate that it remains to be seen how the possible loss of a war in Southeast Asia, or a serious economic depression at home, or the possible exploitation of latent feelings of hostility and prejudice against minorities by persons in

Table IV-6.   Acceptance of Anti-Semitic Beliefs on
Selznick-Steinberg Index, 1969

Belief	Least Anti-Semitic Third	Middle Anti-Semitic Third	Most Anti-Semitic Third	Total
Have too much power in the United States	0%	2%	27%	11%
Care only about their own kind	1	10	62	26
Not as honest as other businessmen	1	16	60	28
Have too much power in the business world	2	20	60	29
More loyal to Israel than to America	2	23	60	30
Control international banking	5	26	54	30
Shrewd and tricky in business	2	20	77	35
Have a lot of irritating faults	6	36	72	40
Use shady practices to get what they want	3	37	81	42
Stick together too much	14	50	86	52
Always like to head things	12	56	88	54

Adapted from Gertrude J. Selznick and Stephen Steinberg, *The Tenacity of Prejudice: Anti-Semitism in Contemporary America* (New York, 1969), p. 28.

public office, or an anti-Israel campaign by the New Left could or would affect the level of anti-Semitism or the status of the Jewish community in the United States.

BLACK ANTI-SEMITISM

There has been much discussion in the past few years—especially since the summer of 1964, when there were extensive Negro riots in cities with large Jewish populations—of increasing amounts of Negro anti-Semitism and of Negroes being more anti-Semitic than whites. Since this topic has evoked such widespread and heated discussion within the past decade, we comment upon it briefly and note it as a special aspect of the general phenomena of attitudes toward Jews in American society. The major source of national poll data available on this topic comes from the study by Gary Marx (1967).

At the outset of his study, Marx listed three alternative expectations about Negro anti-Semitism (p. 127):

1. That it is equally common among Negroes and whites because it stems from the same cultural sources.
2. That Negroes have a special set of grievances against Jews which makes them dislike Jews more than they dislike other whites.
3. That a special affinity between Jews and Negroes makes them less anti-Semitic than whites, and indeed to prefer Jews to other whites.

In the course of his analysis, Marx discarded the second expectation and concluded about the third that while Negroes are no more anti-Semitic than whites, neither do they have any special affinity toward Jews. In other words, Marx found the first expectation to be most congruent with the results obtained from his survey. Some of the data that served to substantiate this conclusion are provided below, and discussed briefly.

One of the major quantitative measures that Marx employed for determining how much anti-Semitism there was among Negroes consisted of an index composed of nine items, seven of which were identical to those used in the Selznick-Steinberg study. Table IV-7

Table IV-7.   Index of Anti-Semitism among Whites and Negroes, 1967

Statement	Anti-Semitic Percentage	
	Whites	*Negroes*
1. Jews have too much power in the United States.	11%	12%
2. Jews have too much power in the business world.	26	26
3. Jews are more willing than others to use shady practices to get what they want.	28	59
4. Jews are (not) just as honest as other businessmen.	30	29
5. Jews don't care what happens to anyone but their own kind.	40	38
6. Jews stick together too much.	52	43
7. The trouble with Jewish businessmen is that they are so shrewd and tricky that other people don't have a fair chance in competition.	54	44

Adapted from Gary Marx, *Protest and Prejudice* (New York, 1967), pp. 128–129, and Gertrude J. Selznick and Stephen Steinberg, *The Tenacity of Prejudice: Anti-Semitism in Contemporary America* (New York, 1969), p. 28.

shows white and Negro responses in 1946 to those seven comparable items. On four of the seven items there were no differences between white and Negro respondents. Twice as many Negroes perceived Jews as more willing to use shady practices, but more whites believed that Jewish businessmen were not fair competitors and that Jews stuck together too much.

On the issue of whether Negroes who manifest anti-Semitic attitudes are likely to be more antiwhite than other Negroes, Marx analyzed attitudes toward Jews within a context of attitudes toward non-Jewish whites. For example, on each of the items in Table IV-8 Jews were perceived in a more favorable light than were non-Jewish whites.

Table IV-8.   Marx Index of Negro Attitudes toward Jews and Non-Jewish Whites, 1967

Item	Jews Better / Easier	Jews Worse / Harder	About the Same	Don't Know
1. Is it better to work for a Jewish person or for a white person who is not Jewish?	34%	19%	10%	37%
2. Would you say that Jewish landlords are better or worse than white landlords who are not Jewish?	24	7	32	37
3. Compared to other white store owners, do you think Jewish store owners are better, worse, or about the same?	20	7	68	5
4. Is it easier to get credit in Jewish or in non-Jewish white-owned stores?	62	9	5	24
5. Are Jews harder or easier than other white store owners on people who fall behind in their payments?	49	16	16	19

Adapted from Gary Marx, *Protest and Prejudice* (New York, 1967), pp. 137, 163.

A good summary table of the findings from the various items used by Marx to obtain measures of anti-Semitic and antiwhite attitudes is shown in Table IV-9. Of the respondents, 13 percent had

Table IV-9. Marx Typology of Negro Hostility toward
Jews and Whites in General, 1967

Score on Anti-Semitism Index	Score on Antiwhite Index			
	Not Anti-white	Low on Antiwhite Hostility	Antiwhite	Total
Not anti-Semitic	13%	19%	4%	36%
Low on anti-Semitism	10	20	11	41
Anti-Semitic	4	10	9	23
Total	27%	49%	24%	100%

Adapted from Gary Marx, *Protest and Prejudice* (New York, 1967), p. 182.

scores which indicated they were neither antiwhite nor anti-Semitic, and 9 percent had scores indicating that they were both antiwhite and anti-Semitic. Only 4 percent were anti-Semitic but not hostile to whites in general, and the same proportion were antiwhite but not anti-Semitic. Of the remaining 70 percent, six out of seven scored low on one or both indices.

Although the information contained in Marx's study was widely disseminated and evoked much discussion, it did not lay to rest the question of how much anti-Semitism existed within the Negro community and whether the phenomenon was spreading. Since the late 1960's, there has been a much-publicized alignment between the leadership of the Black Panthers in the United States and the various Palestinian people's movements in the Middle East. A by-product of that alignment has been the appearance of various publications that, under the guise of attacking the Zionist movement and the state of Israel, are strongly anti-Semitic tracts.

GERMAN JEWRY AND DISPLACED PERSONS

In this section, we shift the focus to review public attitudes toward the Nazis' treatment of Jews in Germany during the 1930's and early 1940's.

The first piece of legislation against the Jews in Germany was passed in April 1933, when a law for "the restoration of the civil service" terminated Jewish participation in a large area of professional, commercial, and cultural life. In September 1935, the Nuremberg laws were passed, which decreed that German citizenship was to be confined to Aryan persons. Non-Aryans were reduced to the status of subjects. Sexual relationships, marital or extramarital, between Jews and Germans were forbidden. German women under the age of 45 could not be employed as servants in Jewish houses. Between 1935 and 1938, an additional thirteen anti-Jewish decrees were passed (Sykes, 1965, p. 164). According to Sykes, by 1938 it was "virtually impossible for a Jew to earn a living in Germany except in the lowest occupations and then only with difficulty."

But in January 1936, Nazi policy on the "Jewish question" had received relatively little publicity in the mass media in the United States. It was not a topic of enormous interest to most Americans, who were struggling through the depression. In the winter of 1936 the public was asked if it thought that in the long run Germany would be better off or worse off if it drove out the Jews (FOR). The responses were distributed as follows: Worse off, 56%; Better off, 14%; No opinion, 30%. Among those with an opinion, four times as many believed that Germany would be worse off. But 30 percent had no opinion on the matter.

By the middle and latter part of 1938, more information appeared in the mass media, and between the summer and fall of 1938 the items shown in Table IV-10 appeared on national polls.

Table IV-10.   Persecution of Jews Abroad, 1938 (AIPO and FOR)

Item	Response	
1. Do you think the persecution of the Jews in Europe has been their own fault (AIPO)?	Not at all	31%
	Partly	48
	Entirely	10
	No opinion	11
2. What do you feel is the reason for hostility toward Jewish people here or abroad (FOR)?	Reasons favorable to Jews	13%
	Reasons unfavorable to Jews	43
	External and neutral reasons	16
	Don't know	28
3. Do you approve or disapprove of the Nazis' treatment of the Jews in Germany (AIPO)?	Approve	6%
	Disapprove	94

What is most interesting about the three sets of responses is how poorly Items 1 and 2 predict responses to Item 3. Only 31 percent believed that the Jews in Germany were not at least partly responsible for their own persecution, and more than three times as many offered reasons unfavorable to Jews as reasons favorable to Jews about why they were objects of hostility (both in the United States and abroad). Yet almost everyone (94 percent) disapproved of the Nazis' treatment of the Jews.

This pattern suggests that in a less intense or dramatic form the American public may have been experiencing another "American dilemma," that is, a conflict between expressing opinions that are consistent with the American ideal of equality and justice and stifling expressions that reflect deeply felt prejudices, ambivalences, and desires to discriminate against Jews. Thus, on the one hand, when asked directly whether they approved of a government's policy of discrimination and persecution because of race or religion, almost everyone answered in the negative. But, on the other hand, when given opportunities to express doubts or ambivalences, or to assess blame without explicitly condoning persecution on religious or racial grounds, a majority was willing to do so.

We also see manifestations of this ambivalence in the public's responses to questions on whether the United States ought to have opened its ports to Jewish refugees who were victims of Nazi policies. It is important, particularly in this context, to remember that the United States was experiencing the most severe economic depression in its history. The likelihood that the American public would have welcomed a large number of immigrants during this period, whatever their race or nationality, who would certainly compete for the same scarce jobs and other resources, is doubtful. Thus, 71 percent answered "no" when asked:

> Should we allow a large number of Jewish exiles from Germany to come to the United States to live (AIPO)?

This figure must be viewed not only as a measure of prejudice toward Jews but as a reflection of the labor market and the state of the economy.

A purer measure of the public's attitudes toward Jewish immigrants may be obtained from responses to the following item:

> Here is a list of different groups of people. Do you think we should let a certain number of each of these groups come to the United States to live after the war, or do you

think we should stop some of the groups from coming at all (NORC)?

IV-2. Percent Willing to Admit Various Groups to United States, 1941 (NORC)

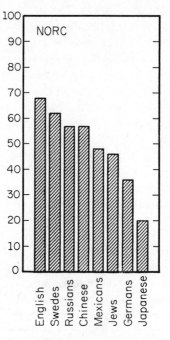

Graph IV-2 shows the public's responses. It is the relative position of the Jews that is so interesting in these responses. This question was asked just before the United States was about to enter the war against Germany and Japan. In comparing Jews against others, we note that they are directly above Germans and Japanese and below any "European" people. Chinese, against whom the United States had exclusionary policies, were viewed as more desirable than Jews. Mexicans, against whom the United States had also instituted stringent quotas, were at least as desirable as Jews.

The items in Table IV-11 are representative of those included in national surveys about the Nazis' treatment of the Jews during World War II. The distribution of responses to these items demonstrates the same sense of ambivalence that the public indicated about

**Table IV-11.   Nazis' Treatment of Jews, 1942-1944
(OPOR and AIPO)**

Item	Response	
1. Do you think Hitler did the		*1942*
right thing when he took away	Yes	17%
the power of the Jews in	No	62
Germany (OPOR)?	Qualified	4
	Don't know / No answer	17
2. Do you think it was a good		*1942*
idea for Hitlet to do this	Yes	14%
(OPOR)?	No	58
	Qualified	8
	Don't know / No answer	20
3. It is said that two million Jews		*1943*
have been killed in Europe	True	47%
since the war began. Do you	Rumor	29
think this is true or just a	No opinion	24
rumor (AIPO)?		
4. Why do you think Hitler took		*1944*
away the power of the Jews in	Sympathetic or neutral reasons	25%
Germany (OPOR)?	Anti-Semitic reasons	49
	Other	4
	No opinion	26
	Total	104%*

*Some persons gave more than one reason.

Hitler's treatment of the Jews in the items on the prewar surveys. While about four times as many did not believe Hitler did the right thing vis-à-vis the Jews or that it was a good idea, the absolute percentages are not all that high. The sizable percentage of "Don't know *or* No answer" responses to these items suggests at least some support for the Nazi program. The fact that 53 percent either discounted as rumor or had no opinion about the two million Jews killed is stronger evidence of ambivalence or unwillingness to believe what must have been a conservative estimate even as early as 1943. Finally, when we look at responses to the fourth item, we note that 49 percent (twice as many respondents) gave reasons that coders categorized as "unsympathetic or anti-Semitic" for Hitler's taking away the power of the Jews in Germany. (Examples of such reasons were "Jews were running the economy" and "Jews have too much power.")

When the findings presented in the first part of this chapter are compared with the responses described above, it appears that the Nazis' treatment of European Jewry did not significantly affect American attitudes toward Jews in the United States. In the trend data reported earlier, we noted that the sharp drop in anti-Semitic responses did not come immediately after World War II, when, if sympathy for the suffering of European Jewry was to be a significant factor, it should have occurred. Instead, the drop occurred in the early 1960's, a decade and a half after the end of the war.

In the same context, we note that in 1961 the American public was asked:

1. In your opinion, is it a good thing or a bad thing for the world to be *reminded* of the horrors of the Nazi concentration camps (AIPO)?
2. Has the Eichmann trial made you feel more or less sympathetic to Israel and the Jewish people (AIPO)?

In response to the first item, 60 percent said that it was a good thing; but 59 percent said that the Eichmann trial had no effect on their feeling toward the Jewish people. These responses came when anti-Semitic attitudes in the United States had dropped to the level to which Stember (1966, p. 217) referred when he wrote "in both feeling and behavior toward Jews, our society has undergone a profound change within the span of one generation."

Even though the United States emerged from World War II determined to play an active role in international politics and not to envelop itself in the blanket of isolationism that had characterized its stance after World War I, its internationalism did not extend to opening its door to refugees of the Nazi holocaust. In the fall of 1945, President Truman proposed legislation that would have bypassed restrictive immigration quotas and permitted refugees in large numbers to enter the United States. The reception that proposed policy received from the American public is shown in part by its responses to the items in Table IV-12. The American people supported massive programs of foreign aid to Western and Central Europe, but most of them were unwilling to alter the restrictive immigration policies established during the 1920's and 1930's, when a depressed economy and an overabundant labor market were cited as the major reasons for such a policy.

Table IV-12. Admittance of European Refugees, 1945-1946 (AIPO)

Item	Response		
1. Would you approve or disapprove of a plan to require *each nation* to take a given number of Jewish and other European refugees, based upon the size and population of each nation?	Approve Disapprove No opinion		*1946* 37% 48 15
2. President Truman plans to ask Congress to allow more Jewish and other European refugees to come to the United States to live than are allowed to under the law now. Would you approve or disapprove of this idea?	Approve Disapprove No opinion		*1946* 16% 72 12
3. About a million Polish people, Jewish, and other displaced persons must find new homes in different countries. Do you think the United States should take *any* of these displaced persons?	Yes No No opinion	*1945* 43% 50 7	*1946* 23% 71 6

THE STATE OF ISRAEL

In November 1947, the General Assembly of the United Nations voted for a partition plan for the former British Mandate of Palestine In 1948, Israel declared its independence and the Kingdom of Transjordan annexed part of Palestine, becoming the Kingdom of Jordan. In the same action, the United Nations also declared that 150,000 Jews, most of whom were waiting in camps on the island of Cyprus or were still in displaced-person centers on the continent of Europe would be permitted entry into the Jewish state. The government of the United States was the first nation to grant official recognition to the state of Israel. The Soviet Union was the second. Right after the United Nations vote, a national survey included the items shown in Table IV-13. It is clear from the responses that the Middle East was not an area of great concern or interest to the American public after World War II. Most respondents favored dismantling the British Mandate and establishing two independent states. But only slightly over a third were willing to state, explicitly, that they sympathized with either the Jews or the Arabs. Two-thirds said they were neutral or had no opinion.

Table IV-13.   Creation of Jewish and Arab States from
Palestine, 1947 (AIPO)

Item	Response	
1. The United Nations has recommended that Palestine be divided into two states, one for the Arabs and one for the Jews and that 150,000 Jews be permitted now to enter the Jewish state. Do you favor or oppose this idea?	Favor	65%
	Oppose	10
	No opinion	25
2. If war breaks out between Arabs and Jews in Palestine, which side would you sympathize with?	Jews	24%
	Arabs	12
	Neutral	38
	No opinion	26

War did break out immediately following the United Nations action and it lasted for over a year. Six months after the fighting started, the public was asked again for its opinion of the United Nations decision. In December 1947, 65 percent had said they favored it. Six months later, the distribution of responses looked like this: Approve of partition, 26%; Try some other solution, 31%; No opinion, 43%. Support had dropped from 65 to 26 percent. At the same time, 90 percent said they had supported the embargo on arms shipments to either Arabs or Jews that the United States had instituted (NORC). Thus, three years after the end of World War II, presumably when knowledge and memories of the Nazis' policy vis-à-vis the Jews were still fresh in the public's mind, and when six months earlier 65 percent said they favored the establishment of a Jewish state, there was a sharp drop in both interest and support.

These findings about the public's attitudes in 1947 and 1948 toward the establishment of a Jewish state in the Middle East support the impression that the experience of European Jewry did little to influence beliefs or attitudes either toward the American Jewish community or toward the Jewish question on the international level. We know, however, that attitudes toward the American Jewish community did change such that there was a sharp decrease in anti-Semitic sentiments in the 1950's and 1960's. The data shown in Graph IV-3 provide one illustration of the magnitude of the change.

The lack of relationship, however, between the holocaust in Europe in the 1930's and 1940's and attitudes toward the American Jewish community does not preclude the absence of a relationship

IV-3.   Percent Hearing Criticism of Jews in Past Six Months, 1940–1959 (AIPO and NORC)

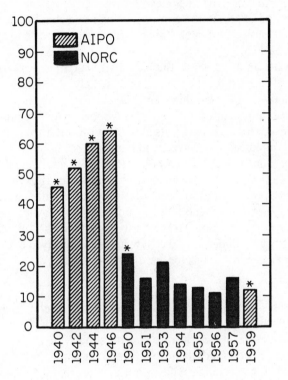

between how Israel fares with its Arab neighbors and attitudes toward American Jewry at the present time. If the American public is persuaded that the state of Israel is the major obstacle to peace in the Middle East and thereby a threat to international peace (for example, because of Israel's refusal to abide by the United Nations 1967 resolution ordering it to return to its pre-1967 borders), attitudes toward the Jews in the United States who support the state of Israel may change. And that change could precipitate a significant increase in anti-Semitism.

Lipset (1971) has emphasized the pervasiveness of anti-Semitism among the New Left, primarily in the United States but in Western Europe as well. He argues that for various reasons Israel is perceived by the New Left as imperialistic, racist, and aggressive. Two of the major reasons for these associations are that Israel is aligned with the United States (and the United States because of Vietnam has become the epitome of evil) and that Israel does not enjoy the support of such "progressive" regimes as China, North Korea, and Cuba.

In denouncing Israel, the New Left also attacks an important source of support for the Jewish state, namely, the American Jewish community. American Jews are blamed for the policies that the Jewish state pursues vis-à-vis the neighboring Arab countries and the Palestinians and also for its identification with the establishment in the United States. A generation ago, leftists could identify with Jews, because Jews, like Negroes or Puerto Ricans, were the under-dogs. Today the American Jewish community, by virtue of its economic position and social status, is part of the affluent establishment. In part out of its desire to gain acceptance by militant black groups who have adopted a pro-Arab line and in part out of its need to identify with underdogs, the New Left feels betrayed by American Jews who can no longer be used as a symbol of a discriminated minority.

At the present time the New Left is not a major political force and its anti-Semitism is not likely to have serious consequences for the American Jewish community. But should the United States suffer a defeat in Southeast Asia or should there be a serious economic depression, then the New Left may find that it has acquired new and potent allies among forces that have a history of anti-Semitic activities and sentiments.

SUGGESTED READINGS

Adorno, T. W., *et al. The Authoritarian Personality.* New York, 1964.

Allport, Gordon. *The Nature of Prejudice.* New York, 1958.

Bettelheim, Bruno, and Morris Janowitz. *Social Change and Prejudice.* Glencoe, Ill., 1964.

Glock, Charles, *et al. The Apathetic Majority.* New York, 1966.

Gordon, Milton. *Assimilation in American Life.* New York, 1964.

Lipset, Seymour Martin. *Anti-Semitism in the United States.* A talk in Jerusalem, March 1971.

Marx, Gary. *Protest and Prejudice.* New York, 1967.

Selznick, Gertrude J., and Stephen Steinberg. *The Tenacity of Prejudice: Anti-Semitism in Contemporary America.* New York, 1969.

Simmel, Ernest, ed. *Anti-Semitism: A Social Disease.* New York, 1946.

Sklare, Marshall. *The Jews: Social Patterns of an American Group.* Glencoe, Ill., 1958.

Stember, Clarles H., *et al. Jews in the Mind of America.* New York, 1966.

Sykes, Christopher. *Cross Roads to Israel.* London, 1965.

Tull, Charles J. *Father Coughlin and the New Deal.* Syracuse, 1965.

Tumin, Melvin. *Inventory and Appraisal of Research on American Anti-Semitism.* New York, 1961.

V
CIVIL LIBERTIES

There is no shortage of either tradition or legal safeguards for protecting the rights of free speech, press, assembly, religion, dissent, protest, and other freedoms associated with civil liberties in American society. Many of these rights are detailed in the federal constitution in the form of the first ten amendments, in state constitutions, or in federal statutes. They have withstood the strains and tensions that have accompanied the shift from an agrarian, rural, relatively homogeneous, isolationist society to an industrial, urban, ethnically diverse one with international commitments. Many Americans consider the civil liberties they enjoy standards by which they judge the quality of government in other nations. It is usually with a good deal of pride that they compare their own system against others.

This chapter considers public opinion about three aspects of civil liberties. First, it reviews public support for freedom of speech and of the press theoretically or in an abstract sense, and then also when specific conditions or contexts are imposed. Second, it reviews the public's response to issues of loyalty and political deviation and expectations concerning political conformity. Third, it reports public support for the right to dissent and demonstrate.

Before we investigate the first theme, it is interesting to note how extensively the topic of civil liberties has been studied by the national polling agencies, who presumably to some degree reflect public interest and concern. Table V-1 lists the number of questions dealing with freedom of speech and dissent over the three decades

**Table V–1.   Number of Items on
Freedom of Speech in Polls,
1936–1970**

Period	Number of Items
1936–1940	9
1941–1945	10
1946–1950	4
1951–1955	9
1956–1960	2
1961–1965	3
1966–1970	7
Total	44

included in this study (*Public Opinion Quarterly*, 1970, p. 483). The distribution shows that interest in the topic increased during periods of heightened tension or national emergency, as witness the number of items that appeared from 1936 to 1945, 1951 to 1955 (the Korean War and McCarthyism), and 1966 to 1970 (the war in Vietnam). During periods of relative stability and quiescence, interest in the topic drops off noticeably.

FREEDOM OF SPEECH AND THE PRESS

On the issue of free speech the public seemed to respond variably, depending on the conditions imposed by the specific question. For example, when an item was worded in a general or theoretical form, "Do you believe in freedom of speech?" almost everyone (that is, over 96 percent) answered "yes" (OPOR). We say "seemed" because unfortunately that wording was used only in 1938 and 1940. After that, whenever the issue of free speech was posed, special conditions or limitations were attached. For example, before World War II, the public was asked two kinds of questions pertaining to free speech. The first item was asked of the 96 percent who answered that they believed in freedom of speech. The responses are shown in Table V–2. Between one-half and three-quarters of the 96 percent who had answered "yes" to the question "Do you believe in free speech?" also favored limiting that right or prohibiting it under the conditions imposed by the above questions.

**Table V-2.   Unlimited Freedom of Speech, 1938-1941
(OPOR, AIPO, and ROP)**

Item	Year	Favor/ Unlimited	Oppose/ Limited	No Opinion
1. Do you believe in it (freedom of speech) to the extent of allowing radicals to hold meetings and express their views in this community?	1938 (OPOR)	38%	61%	1%
	1940 (AIPO)	22	76	2
2. Do you think that in America anybody should be allowed to speak on any subject any time he wants to, or do you think there are times when free speech should be pronibited or certain subjects or speakers prohibited?	1940 (ROP)	49%	44%	7%
	1941 (OPOR)	44	53	3

During World War II and in the decade after it, the public was asked whether in peacetime people should be allowed to say "anything they want in a public speech." The percentage who answered "yes" in the various years were: 1943, 63%; 1945, 64%; 1946, 64%; 1949, 50%; 1953, 53%; 1954, 56%. In 1949, 1953, and 1954, the question was worded and the responses coded somewhat differently. Both factors probably account for the differences in percentage between the earlier and later periods.

More recently in 1970, the public was asked whether it thought everyone should have the right to criticize the government, even if the criticism were damaging to national interests: 42 percent said "yes," 54 percent "no", and 4 percent "no opinion" (CBS).

Over the span of three decades from 1940 to 1970, the public was consistent in its response to the issue of freedom of speech. Most respondents favored it, but not unequivocally. The 96 percent who answered "yes" to the more abstract or theoretical phrasing of the question would not be a useful proxy for describing the public's support of free speech in real situations. It would be more accurate to say that most people favored imposing limitations and conditions on freedom of speech that served the national interest and that prohibited radical expressions or sentiments.

The public's responses to a closely related topic, but one for which the data do not span as long a time period, is freedom of the press. In the period preceding World War II and the immediate postwar years, the public was asked its opinion of newspapers criticizing our form of government and whether the Socialist Party should be allowed to publish a newspaper. Responses are shown in Table V-3. The pattern is similar to the one reported for the items

Table V-3. **Unlimited Freedom of the Press, 1936-1954 (NORC and AIPO)**

Item	Year	Yes	Qualified Yes	No	Undecided
1. (In peacetime) do you	1936*	52%	—	42%	6%
think newspapers	1937*	55	—	39	6
should be allowed to	1943	66	—	30	4
criticize our form of	1944	66	—	30	4
government (NORC)?	1946	66	—	30	4
	1948	70	—	27	3
	1953	57	7	35	4
2. Do you think the	1943	57%	—	25%	18%
Socialist Party should be	1944	57	—	25	18
allowed to publish	1946	58	—	26	16
newspapers in this	1953	45	5	†	†
country (NORC)?	1954	40	5	†	†

*In 1936 and 1937, the items were worded somewhat differently, but the substance was sufficiently comparable so that the results may be included in the figures shown above. In 1936, the question read: "Do you think the press should have the right to say anything it pleases about public officials (AIPO)?" In 1937, the question read: "Do you think newspapers should be allowed to print anything they choose except libelous matter (AIPO)?"
†Not available.

on free speech. By no means does freedom of the press have the unequivocal and universal support of the American public. For example, about half opposed the right to print its ideas of a relatively moderate, nonviolent, political press that espouses democratic socialism of the variety periodically voted into office in Great Britain, and one-third opposed the right of a free press as guaranteed by the first amendment to the federal constitution.

LOYALTY AND CONFORMITY

Shortly after the onset of the cold war, and the McCarthy era,[1] both of which occurred in the late 1940's and early 1950's, the loyalties and judgments of many different types of people became suspect: government bureaucrats, elected officials, members of the diplomatic corps, labor officials, academics, persons in all phases and levels of public life. In many instances, traditional rules of procedure concerning burdens of proof, rules of evidence, and the like were either bent to support political objectives or simply ignored.

Senator McCarthy, with the support of other members of his party, notably Senator Karl Mundt and Congressman Richard Nixon, held Congressional hearings, made speeches, and sponsored legislation the aims of which were to tighten internal security, to locate and dismiss government employees whose loyalties were considered doubtful or who might be serving the interests of a foreign government, to impress on the American public the dangers of internal subversion, the need for evidence of loyalty on the part of government employees, professors, labor officials, the clergy, and others, and the importance of vigilance in matters of national security.

Before we examine the public's response to these objectives, we should know something of its reaction to the charges made by the junior senator from Wisconsin. On February 9, 1950, Senator McCarthy, in a speech delivered in Wheeling, West Virginia, declared that the State Department was currently employing 207 Communists. Eleven days later, when the Senator read his Wheeling speech into the Congressional record, he altered the number of Communists from 207 to 57.

In the summer of 1950, the public was asked whether it thought that Senator McCarthy's charges were doing the country more harm than good and whether it had heard or read about Senator McCarthy's charges that there were Communists in the State Department.[2] If the respondent answered that he had, he was asked

---

[1] Named after the junior senator from Wisconsin. Joseph K. McCarthy, who had embarked on a career of publicizing and exposing Communist Party members or communist sympathizers in universities and government agencies.

[2] The items were asked of the 84 percent who said in a previous item that they had heard of Senator McCarthy.

for his opinion of these charges. The responses to the first item, about the effect on the country of Senator McCarthy's charges were: More good, 39%; More harm, 29%; No opinion, 16%; Unfamiliar, 16% (AIPO). The public's opinion of McCarthy's charges was: Approval, 31%; Qualified approval, 10%; Disapproval, 20%; On the fence, 6%; No opinion, 11%; Haven't heard of charges, 22% (AIPO). On both items, there was more support for or approval of the Senator's actions and charges than there was disapproval. To both, about a third of the respondents had either not heard of the charges or did not wish to express an opinion (perhaps because they were unfamiliar with the problem). Looking only at the responses of those with an opinion, we find that 57 percent compared to 43 percent believed that Senator McCarthy's charges were doing the country more good than harm; and 61 percent compared to 30 percent approved (with some qualifications) of the Senator's charges about Communists in the State Department. Brief and somewhat superficial as these data are, they indicate that Senator McCarthy's activities were not going unnoticed; nor were they meeting with widespread disapproval.

In 1947, in response to Congressional insistence that the government "tighten its loyalty procedures," President Truman issued an executive order that essentially revamped the entire security program by providing greater centralized authority and removing ultimate responsibility from heads of individual agencies whose standards tended to vary. In the summer of 1948, Congress passed the Mundt-Nixon bill, which required members of the Communist Party to register with the Justice Department. During debate over the bill, the public was asked whether the Congress ought to pass it and 63 percent answered "yes" (AIPO). A year or two later, when asked whether they favored registration of Communist Party members, a large majority said they did (AIPO):

	Yes	*No*	*No Opinion*
1949	80%	10%	10%
1950	67	20	13

During this same period, between 1946 and 1948, the public was asked how it thought Communist Party members would behave should war break out between the United States and Russia (AIPO). On each of three surveys, of those with an opinion (between 29 and

21 percent did not have an opinion), more than twice as many thought that Communist Party members in the United States would be loyal to Russia.

As the cold war between the United States and the Soviet Union grew more intense, the range of acceptable activities for persons who acknowledged membership in the Communist Party diminished. For example, in September 1950, Congress passed an internal-security act (over a Presidential veto) that required all communist organizations including so-called front groups to register with the Attorney General and to furnish the Justice Department with a list of its members. Communists were barred from employment in defense plants, denied passports for travel, and subject to internment in case of war.

The items and responses shown in Table V–4 describe public opinion concerning the activities that Communist Party members

Table V–4.   Permissible Activities of Communist Party Members, 1949–1950 (AIPO)

Item	Response	1949	1950
1. Do you think all communists should or should not be removed from jobs in United States industries that would be important in wartime?	Should be removed	87%	90%
2. Some people say that as long as the Communist Party is permitted by law in the United States, colleges and university teachers should be allowed to belong to the party and to continue teaching. Do you agree or disagree?	Disagree	73%	
3. The University of California recently said it would require all its teachers to take an oath that they are not communists. Some other colleges oppose this idea because they feel it is an insult to teachers to require them to take such an oath. How do you feel about this?	Agree with University of California	70%	

ought to be permitted to engage in during this period. On each item at least 70 percent answered in the direction that advocated placing restrictions on the activities of admitted communists.

However, the public did distinguish between persons who were accused of communist ties and admitted party members. For example, in 1947, when asked the following question, almost three times as many favored allowing an employee to present his case as did those who said fire him:

> If questions of national security are involved, should our government have the right to fire employees at any time if their dependability or loyalty to the United States is questioned—or should every United States Government employee have the right to present his side of the case (AIPO)?

Fire Him	*Present His Case*	*No Opinion*
24%	68%	8%

The following item was also asked in the fall of 1947, and while the results are not as clear-cut as in the item above, the direction is the same. The responses are shown in Table V-5. We can assume from the greater proportion of no-opinion responses made to this item, as opposed to the previous one about the right of an employee to present his case, that the public found the problem posed in this question a more difficult one. We note also that the public was more willing to have persons suspected of having communist sympathies work in a large corporation than in a labor union.

> Do you believe that there *should* or should *not* be a law preventing *people suspected of communist sympathies* from holding any kind of *public office*; an executive position in a *labor union*; a job in *a large corporation* (AIPO)?

Table V-5. Law Barring Suspected Communists from Various Occupations, 1947 (AIPO)

Occupation	*Favor*	*Oppose*	*No Opinion*
Public office	36%	41%	23%
Executive position in labor union	37	40	23
Job in large corporation	28	47	25

Labor unions were more suspect than most institutions during this period. Even before internal pressures developed to "clean out

**Table V–6. Extent of Preference for Russian System in
Various Occupations, 1946 (AIPO)**

Occupation	Many	Few	None	Don't Know
Labor-union leaders	19%	29%	22%	30%
People with government jobs	6	26	35	33
School teachers	4	25	37	34
Newspapermen	3	34	38	25
Radio commentators	3	28	44	25

the reds and pinks," the public expressed concern that the trade
unions were "hotbeds" of communist activity. When asked the
following question in the summer of 1946, the public responded as
shown in Table V–6. By a ratio of three to one, labor leaders were
considered more sympathetic toward the Soviet Union than were
school teachers, government workers, or mass-media employees.

> Is it your impression that a good many, relatively few, or
> practically no radio commentators, newspapermen,
> labor-union leaders, school teachers, people with govern-
> ment jobs in Washington believe that the Russian system
> is better than ours (AIPO)?

When asked directly about the extent of communist activity or
support for communism in the unions, the answers were distributed
as follows: Great amount, 38%; Fair amount, 27%; Small amount,
16%; None *or* No opinion, 19% (AIPO). A few months after this
poll was conducted, the Taft-Hartley Act was debated in the
Congress. Another poll which was conducted shortly after the
debate revealed that the anticommunist provisions of the Taft-
Hartley Act received particularly strong popular support. Over 80
percent of the public said they "approved of a law that required
employers and officers in labor unions to swear that they are not
communists before they could take a case before the National Labor
Relations Board" (AIPO).

In 1953, in response to the growing concerns voiced by various
funding agencies, civic organizations, and the American Civil
Liberties Union that important democratic beliefs and practices
were seriously threatened and that the activities of political groups
and individuals were impeded by Congressional investigations and
loyalty probes, the Carnegie Foundation sponsored a national

survey to assess the political mood of the country (published in Stouffer, 1957). More specifically, the purpose of the survey was to find out to what extent the rank and file of Americans supported the emphasis advocated by McCarthy on political and social conformity.

Graphs V–1, V–2, and V–3, prepared from the data reported in Stouffer (1957), describe the public's responses to the rights of socialists, atheists, communists, and persons whose loyalties have been questioned but who denied the allegations against them to make a speech, have a book in the public library, and hold a teaching job. Of the four types of people, the public was most willing to acknowledge the rights of the socialist and least willing to acknowledge those of the communist. The atheist was more suspect than the man whose loyalty had been questioned on grounds that he might be a communist. Of the three types of activities, making a public speech was more likely to be tolerated than retaining a book in the

V–1. Percent Allowing Socialist, Atheist, Person of Suspect Loyalty, and Communist to Make a Speech. 1953–1954 (Carnegie Foundation)

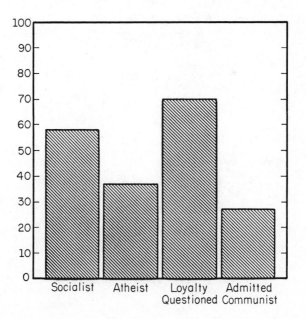

V-2.   Percent Opposed to Removing from Library a Book by Socialist, Atheist, and Communist, 1953-1954 (Carnegie Foundation)

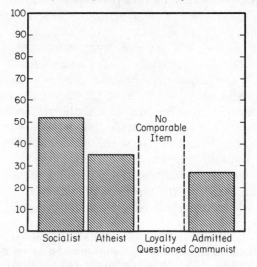

V-3.   Percent Allowing Socialist, Atheist, Person of Suspect Loyalty, and Communist to Teach, 1953-1954 (Carnegie Foundation)

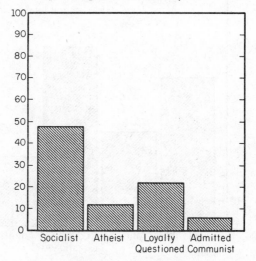

library authored by a person with radical or deviant political views or permitting him to teach in a college or university. The public speech is a one-shot affair that might be important symbolically but is less likely to have long-term negative or dangerous consequences. It is also more difficult to limit or control the effects of someone's teachings or writings than it is his public statements on a single occasion.

Table V-7. Dismissal of Communist and Person of Suspect Loyalty, 1953-1954 (Carnegie Foundation)

Item		Person of Suspect Loyalty	Admitted Communist
1. Suppose this man is a high-	No	69%	5%
school teacher, should he	Yes	22	91
be fired or not?	No opinion	9	4
2. Suppose he has been working	No	72%	6%
in a defense plant, should	Yes	18	90
he be fired or not?	No opinion	10	4
3. Suppose he is a clerk in a	No	81%	26%
store, should he be fired	Yes	11	68
or not?	No opinion	8	6
4. Suppose he is a radio singer,	No	80%	29%
should he be fired or not?	Yes	12	63
	No opinion	8	8

In Table V-7 are some additional items from the Carnegie Foundation survey that emphasize even more clearly the sharp distinction the public made between a man whose loyalty is questioned on grounds that he might be a communist and an admitted communist. Public sentiment favored denying the admitted communist the right to work not only in "sensitive areas" but in all types of gainful employment. In contrast, only a small proportion of the respondents favored restricting the rights of the man whose loyalty had been questioned to work even at a job where security might be of some significance.

During this same period, 1953-1954, the public was also asked about the kinds of behavior that would appear suspect in its eyes. The responses presented in Table V-8 show that criticism of American society was not per se grounds for suspicion of disloyalty. Rather, an overt act, such as attendance at a Communist Party meeting or refusal to sign a loyalty oath, needed to be committed before a person's loyalty became suspect. This differentiation is illustrated by the responses in Table V-8 to the following question (adapted from Stouffer, 1957).

> Would you yourself be *very* suspicious that he was a communist, or just a little suspicious, or wouldn't you suspect him at all just because of that [criticizing American society] (Carnegie Foundation)?

Table V-8.   Extent of Suspicion of Various Behaviors as Indicators of Disloyalty, 1953-1954 (Carnegie Foundation)

Behavior	Great	Slight	None	Don't Know
1. A person who goes around talking against religion	16%	28%	53%	3%
2. A person who refuses to sign an oath of loyalty to the United States	63	26	8	3
3. A person who goes around criticizing conditions in this country	15	28	52	5
4. A person who signs a petition saying we should never use the atom bomb	15	25	53	7
5. A person who goes to a Communist Party meeting	65	22	9	4
6. A teacher who tells his students that there are many things wrong in America	34	32	30	4

Perhaps the strongest expression of public censure of domestic communists during this period was reflected in the fact that 77 percent said they favored revoking the citizenship of admitted communists; 51 percent said that "anyone who admitted he was a communist ought to be put in jail," and 73 percent believed it was a "good idea for people to report to the Federal Bureau of Investigation any neighbors or acquaintances whom they suspected of being communists" (AIPO). In 1950, when asked: "In the event we get into a war with Russia what, if anything, do you believe should be done about communists in the United States?" 80 percent answered "shoot, deport, or imprison them."

Unfortunately, none of these items pertaining to loyalty and political conformity was repeated in the following decade. There are, therefore, no recent national surveys that report public opinion concerning these issues.

THE RIGHT TO DISSENT AND DEMONSTRATE

Between 1965 and 1970, a few items concerning the right to dissent, particularly within the context of demonstrations against the Vietnam War, appeared on national polls. Responses described in Graph V-4 show the level of support for one manifestation of political dissent in the 1960's.

> Do you think people have the right to conduct peaceful demonstrations against the war in Vietnam (HAR)?

V-4.   Percent Opposing Demonstrations against Vietnam War, 1965–1970 (HAR)

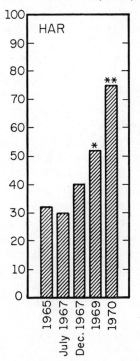

From the evidence, we conclude that the public responded to expressions of political dissent in the 1960's much as they did to the free-speech issue in the 1930's and early 1940's. In concrete situations, when given a choice between manifestations of support for order and conformity versus expressions of dissent and protest, public support for the principle of free expression diminishes sharply. Responses in 1969, and especially in 1970, show a noticeable increase in the proportion who oppose dissent. While the responses to the 1969 item may be explained partly by the public's annoyance with the activities of students, the items that appeared in 1970 did not mention students. The proportion who opposed dissent nevertheless increased by almost 100 percent since 1967, and by almost 70 percent since 1969.

In 1970, 75 percent did not approve of organized peaceful protests against government policy. In 1940, 76 percent opposed the right of radicals to hold meetings and express their opinions. In the interim three decades, when the United States was neither at war nor on the verge of war, and after McCarthyism had subsided, the public exhibited a more relaxed and permissive attitude concerning the right of political radicals.[3] But at no time between 1940 and 1970 did the level of public support approach the 96 percent who said that they favored freedom of speech when asked in an abstract or theoretical form. At best, during periods of relative stability and quiescence, the level of support was between 50 and 60 percent.

We conclude from this discussion that the civil liberties provided and protected by federal and state constitutions and federal statutes do not enjoy strong popular support much of the time and that if they were not protected from recall or revision by enormously complicated mechanisms, such statutes might indeed be in jeopardy. On the other hand, it is also possible that the American public feels free to express punitive and repressive sentiments vis-à-vis the civil liberties of political minorities because it understands implicitly that the rights of free speech and dissent will not be seriously endangered by such perhaps largely "expressive" opinions. But if such a strategy is indeed operative, even implicitly, it is a dangerous course to pursue.

[3] See for example the data on attitudes toward free speech and a free press earlier in this chapter.

SUGGESTED READINGS

Barth, Alan. *The Loyalty of Free Men.* New York, 1952.

Bell, Daniel, ed. *The New American Right.* New York, 1955.

Chafee, Zachariah. *Free Speech in the United States.* Cambridge, 1948.

Gelhorn, Walter. *Individual Freedom and Governmental Restraint.* Baton Rouge, 1956.

Lazarsfeld, Paul F., and Wagner Thielens, Jr. *The Academic Mind: Social Scientists in a Time of Crisis.* Glencoe, Ill., 1958.

Rovere, Richard. *Senator Joseph McCarthy.* New York, 1959.

Shils, Edward A. *The Torment of Secrecy.* Glencoe, Ill., 1956.

Spinrad, William. *Civil Liberties.* Chicago, 1970.

Stouffer, Samuel. *Communism, Conformity and Civil Liberties: A Cross Section of the Nation Speaks Its Mind.* New York, 1955.

VI
FOREIGN POLICY

This chapter traces public opinion on a variety of important issues involving foreign policy from the late 1930's to the end of the 1960's. The enormous number and complexity of issues make it impractical to attempt to report public opinion on all of them. What this chapter sets out to do is to provide data on the public's reactions to those topics that have persisted from one decade to another or to those issues that resulted in crises at particular points in time.

Thus, public reaction to American involvement in the wars that occurred during this period and, in retrospect, to American participation in World War I is reviewed. For the period since World War II, we report attitudes toward former allies and enemies and the support the public expressed for the policies that were pursued vis-à-vis both. The public's reactions to the atomic bomb and the complex issues concerning its use, the distribution of information about atomic energy, and international control of atomic weapons are also reported. The public's response to the massive programs of foreign aid and the international commitments that the United States assumed following World War II is reviewed. Finally, the extent to which the public supported or failed to support the wars of the 1950's and 1960's in Korea and Vietnam is discussed, and reactions to both are compared. In short, the chapter tries to review public opinion and response both to long-standing themes and to crucial one-shot events. It cannot and does not claim to be a comprehensive description of public opinion on all of the issues in American foreign policy over three decades. Admittedly, there are even some issues which at the time they occurred aroused the concern of the government and presumably the public, such as the Cuban missile crisis of 1962, about which we do not provide any data.

For the most part, the data are presented in the chronological order in which the events occurred. In some instances, for purposes of clarity, we consider opinions reported over different periods of time to the same substantive issue.

A few comments, at the outset, about the relationship between foreign policy and public opinion are in order. In Chapter II, we noted that, in contrast to many domestic issues, the formulation and execution of foreign policy comprise an area that many citizens may be more willing to delegate to experts. In this connection, Almond (1950, p. 5) observed:

> There are inherent limitations in modern society on the capacity of the public to understand the issues and grasp the significance of the most important problems of public policy. This is particularly the case with foreign policy where the issues are especially complex and remote.

In his analysis of the public's response to McCarthyism and its potential threat to civil liberties in the early 1950's, Stouffer (1957) emphasized that for most Americans the issues that have the greatest relevance and importance are those that affect their day-to-day lives. Americans, he claimed, are intensely involved in private matters affecting their pocketbooks, their jobs, their children, and their health.

The relative lack of interest in public affairs as compared with private interests is seen most dramatically in the public's response to matters affecting foreign policy. During periods of relative stability, as for example during much of the Eisenhower era, the public was less likely to demand an accounting or an explanation from its elected representatives in the House or the Senate on how they voted on foreign-policy questions as compared to how they voted on farm policy, tax bills, labor legislation, or civil rights. It is during a crisis, such as a war, a threat of war, or news that another nation has tested an atomic bomb for the first time, that the American public becomes mobilized around issues of foreign policy.

Almond believes that because under normal circumstances the American public is indifferent to foreign policy, when an event occurs that is perceived as a threat to national security, the public tends to overreact. He warns that "the volatility and potential explosiveness of American opinion must be constantly kept in mind if panic reactions to threat are to be avoided" (Almond, 1950, p. 55).

Even after 1945, when the mass media and public officials warned of the dangers to national security should the United States again adopt an isolationist course, the public seemed willing to delegate foreign-policy concerns to a back shelf. We note, for example, that when the American Institute of Public Opinion asked the public "What do you regard as the most important problem before the American public today?" between October 1945 and December 1946, the percentage who named foreign problems as most vital ranged from 7 to 23 percent. The announcement of the Truman Doctrine, the Marshall Plan, and the increasing tension between the United States and the Soviet Union raised the proportion answering "foreign policy" in the spring and summer of 1947 to 54 and 47 percent.

Along these same lines, Key (1961, p. 81) described a study by Martin Kriesberg in 1949 in which the latter examined national-poll results on foreign-policy questions and grouped public responses into three categories: "unaware," "aware, but uninformed" and "informed." Kriesberg found that 30 percent were unaware of any given event in American foreign affairs; 45 percent were aware but uninformed (that is, they may have heard of the Marshall Plan, but did not know its purpose); and 25 percent were informed (that is, they could give a reasonably accurate statement about the issue).

The ignorance or indifference of the American public to foreign policy is relative to its interest and awareness of private matters and selected topics in the domestic sphere. One should not conclude, however, on the basis of these observations, that the American public is more or less interested and/or knowledgeable than the public in other nations. But as Almond (1950, p. 81) has commented, "a lack of information on foreign policy problems among the American public may affect policy more significantly in the United States than it would in foreign countries."

Two comments follow from this observation. One is that

ignorance and indifference on the part of the American public may have greater consequences for the rest of the world than would an indifferent or ignorant public of a less powerful nation or one whose government was less responsive to the public's mood. The second comment is that given the varied ethnic composition of the American public, members of which are likely to have special interests or loyalties to specific foreign countries, relative indifference or ignorance on the part of much of the public may provide the opportunity for ethnic groups to exercise greater influence on foreign policy in general, and toward specific countries in particular, than would be likely if the public as a whole were more aware of foreign policy. This is not to say that such influence is in and of itself pernicious or necessarily contrary to the best interests of the United States. It is to say that such influence may commit the United States to friendships or policies that do not reflect the underlying mood of the majority.

With this perspective on the state of the public's interest and attitude toward foreign policy in general, we turn to an examination of substantive issues. We begin with an analysis of the public's attitudes in the 1930's to the turmoil in Europe and to the likelihood of American involvement.

BEFORE WORLD WAR II

Involvement in Previous and Present Conflicts

During the depression decade of the 1930's, the modal response of the American public to the turmoil in Europe and Asia, triggered mainly by the rise of the Nazi Party in Germany and by the militarists' control of Japan, was one of withdrawal and hostility toward any overtures or suggestions of alignments with foreign governments. Not only did the public express dislike for the prospect of involvement in the future, but many respondents indicated that they had reconsidered the worthwhileness of the United States entry into the previous major conflict and believed that it had been a mistake. For example, in 1937, the public was asked:

1. Do you think it was a mistake for the United States to enter the World War (AIPO)?

2. If another war like the World War develops in Europe
should America take part again (AIPO)?

In response, 64 percent said "yes" to the first question, and 95
percent answered "no" to the second. These responses were made in
1937. In retrospect, they represent the high point in the public's
desire to remain detached from European conflicts. By 1937, Hitler
had been chancellor for four years, but the *Anschluss* with Austria
had not yet been made and German troops had not occupied
foreign soil.

**Table VI-1.   United States Entry in World
War I a Mistake, 1937-1941 (AIPO)**

Year	Yes	No	No Opinion
1937	64%	28%	8%
1939	59	28	13
1941	39	42	19

The first item, about the rightness or wrongness of the United
States having entered World War I, reappeared on surveys in 1939
and early in 1941. The distribution of responses at those times compared to 1937 is shown in Table VI-1. The percentage who believed
it was a mistake decreased by 60 percent between 1937 and January
1941. Proportionally, more of them slipped into the "no opinion"
than into the "no, not a mistake" category, indicating that this was a
period of considerable uncertainty and confusion about what
American policy ought to be. By January 1941, almost all of
Western Europe, including France, had been occupied by the
German army and the height of the German blitz over Britain had
occurred just a few months before, in the fall of 1940. The Hitler-
Stalin nonaggression pact was still in effect and the eastern front
was peaceful. January 1941 could have been perceived as a critical
period in the war.

Concerning the second item, about United States involvement
in another war "like the World War," the following item bearing on
that issue appeared on national polls between March 1939 and
October 1941:

Should we send our Army and Navy abroad to fight Germany and Italy (AIPO)?

Between May 1940 and October 1941, this version was used:

If the question of the United States going to war against Germany and Italy came up for a national vote within the next two weeks, would you vote to go into the war or stay out (AIPO)?

Table VI-2. United States Entry in War against Germany and Italy, 1939-1941 (AIPO)

Month and Year	Stay Out
March 1939	83%
September 1939*	84
May 1940	86
January 1941	88
October 1941	79

*It is worth noting that at the same time 84 percent said they would vote to stay out of a war against Germany and Italy, 72 percent answered "yes" to the following question: "If Cuba or any other country within 1,500 miles of the Panama Canal is actually invaded by any European power, do you think the United States should fight to keep the European country out (AIPO)?"

Responses are shown in Table VI-2. Two months before Pearl Harbor (in October 1941), 79 percent said that if given the oppor-·tunity they would vote to stay out of the war. Between March 1939, which was six months before the German invasion of Poland, and October 1941—in other words, after Britain and France had enetered the war and Germany had invaded the Soviet Union and conquered almost all of Western Europe—there was no significant alteration in the public's desire not to become involved again.

The responses reported thus far describe the public's reaction on the dimension on what its government's policy *ought* to be. Graph VI-1 shows responses to the issue of whether or not the United States would be *able* to stay out of another general European war, should one develop. Until the German invasion of Poland in September 1939, which had the effect of bringing France and Britain into the war against Germany, there was a trend that

VI–1.   Percent Saying United States Could Stay Out of War, 1937–1941 (AIPO)

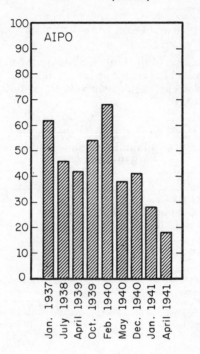

indicated a decline in the proportion who expected that the United States would be able to stay out. For a brief period from October 1939 to February 1940, the direction shifted, such that 54 and 68 percent thought the United States could stay out, probably because they believed Britain and France would be able to defeat Germany. With the fall of France in May 1940, the percentage declined steadily. (The slight reversal in December 1940 is attributable, perhaps, to the success of the Greeks against the Italian invasion.)

We have reported responses on the "should" and "could" dimension. During a part of this same period, the public was also asked, when appropriate:

Do you think the United States *will* stay out of another world war (if there is one) (AIPO)?

VI-2.   Percent Saying United States Would Stay Out of War, 1939-1941 (AIPO)

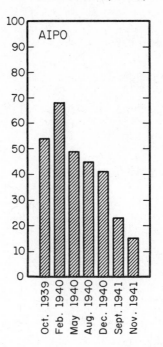

Responses are shown in Graph VI-2. Note that responses on the "could" and "would" dimensions are almost identical. The last time the public was asked whether it thought the United States "could" stay out was April 1941 (which was before Germany invaded the Soviet Union), and at that time only 18 percent thought it could. By November 1941 (less than a month before the Japanese attack on Pearl Harbor), 15 percent said they thought the United States "would" stay out of the war.

So much for general items concerning the stance that the United States should or would be likely to adopt vis-à-vis involvement in the next European war. We shift now to a discussion of the public's attitudes toward questions of strategy and its willingness to support specific nations. The first series of items pertains to Great Britain and France. With some variations, the following question was asked from May 1939 until December 8, 1941, by which time the United States was at war with Germany:

> Should we lend money to England and France to buy airplanes and other war materials in the country (AIPO)?

In January 1940, the question read:

> If it looked as though England and France would lose the war unless we loaned money, would you favor lending money to buy supplies (AIPO)?

In December 1940, the question read:

> Our present neutrality law prevents this country from selling war materials to any country fighting in a declared war. Do you think the law should be changed so that we could sell war materials to England and France in case of war (AIPO)?

	May 1939	*January 1940*	*December 1940*
No	69%	45%	45%

After the fall of France, when Great Britain was the only major power at war with Germany, the public was asked:

> Which of these things do you think is the more important for the United States to try to do—keep out of the war ourselves, or help England win, even at the risk of getting into the war (AIPO)?

	May 1939	*Aug. 1940*	*Jan. 1941*	*May 1941*
Stay out	64%	53%	40%	39%

The responses to both items show a consistent trend in the direction of support for France and Britain, and then after the French defeat, for Britain alone. But even as of May 1941, seven months before Pearl Harbor, and one year after the British had been fighting alone, 39 percent believed that above any other consideration, the United States should not risk getting involved in the war.

Until Germany invaded the Soviet Union in June 1941, supporters in the United States of both the extreme right, who had some sympathy with Nazi ideology, and the extreme left, many of whom identified with the Soviet Union, were adamantly neutral. These elements in the population made common cause with the traditional isolationists, who were not committed to an ideology of the left or the right but who favored as little international involvement as possible even for a nation that was a major world power.

Further insight into the public's beliefs about what the most appropriate role for the United States should be is shown by the responses it selected from among the choices listed in Table VI–3. Through July 1940 the question read:

Which of these courses of action comes closest to describing what you think the United States should do (FOR)?

Table VI–3.   United States Role before and after Fall of France, 1939–1940 (FOR)

Statement	September 1939	December 1939	July 1940
1. Enter the war on the side of England and France only if it looks as if they are losing—in the meantime, help with food and materials	14%	15%	27%*
2. Do not enter the war but supply England and France with materials; refuse to ship to Germany.	20	9	41
3. Take no sides—offer to sell to anyone on a cash-and-carry basis.	29	38	26
4. Refuse aid of any kind to either side.	25	30	—
5. Other / Don't know	12	8	6

*Of this 27 percent, 8 percent would enter on the side of the Allies whether or not they seemed to be losing.

After the fall of France, 27 percent favored entering the war immediately or were prepared to do so and would support such action if the British position appeared hopeless; 26 percent favored maintaining a position of neutrality that would permit the United States to gain financially from the sale of arms and other materials to any nation that had the money to make the purchases. The modal response advocated material support (short of sending troops) to the Allies and an embargo against Germany. (After two months of debate the Congress passed the Lend Lease Act in March 1941, which called for supplying goods to "the enemies of Hitler"; at that time, Great Britain was the major recipient.)

The same type of question, but with different alternatives, was included in a national poll conducted by *Fortune* magazine thirteen months later. The second wave of the poll was conducted only a few days before Pearl Harbor and the subsequent declaration of war against Germany by the United States. The responses to the following question are given in Table VI-4.

Which one of the following statements most nearly represents your attitude towards the present war (FOR)?

Table VI-4.   United States Role before Pearl Harbor, 1941 (FOR)

Statement	August 1941	December 1941
1. Those who think this is our war are wrong, and the people of this country should resist to the last ditch any move that would lead us further toward war.	16%	13%
2. A lot of mistakes have brought us close to a war that isn't ours, but now that it is done, we should support in full the government.	22	28
3. While at first it looked as though this was not our war, it now looks as though we should back England until Hitler is beaten.	42	39
4. It is our war as well as England's and we should have been in there fighting with her before this.	12	15
5. Don't know.	8	5

A matter of days before Pearl Harbor, 15 percent advocated immediate United States entry into the war as England's partner, and about the same proportion (13 percent) advocated unequivocal nonparticipation. While it is somewhat difficult to compare the responses between items because the choices are not the same, it would appear that support for nonparticipation had diminished from 26 to 13 percent, and support for immediate involvement had increased by about the same proportion from 8 to 15 percent between July 1940 and December 1941.

If we examine only the second question—asked shortly before Pearl Harbor—it also appears that two-thirds of the respondents favored the government's lend-lease program at the very least (responses to Alternatives 2 and 3), and more than half as many were willing to go even further toward committing the United States to the Allies' cause. The date of these responses is December 1941.

Nations Involved in Previous and Present Conflicts

We look next at the public's opinion of Germany, beginning in 1937:

> Do you consider any nation or nations chiefly guilty of causing the World War (AIPO)?

In response, 55 percent said "no." The 45 percent who answered "yes" named the following countries: Germany, 77%; France, 5%; Britain, 5%; Austria, 4%; Others, 9% (AIPO).

> Do you think the peace treaty after the war was too easy or too severe on Germany (AIPO)?

The distribution was: Too easy, 41%; Too severe, 30%; About right, 29%.

Responses to both items show that the public, as of 1937, had not reached a consensus about Germany. The 55 percent who did not believe any nation or nations could be designated as chiefly guilty of causing World War I and the 30 percent who believed that the peace treaty following the end of that war was too severe reflect, at the least, a neutral feeling toward Germany and, at the most, an agreement with one of the major premises of the Nazi movement; namely, that Germany had received too harsh treatment at the hands of the Allied powers.

A few months later, in April 1938, which was after the German army occupied Austria, 54 percent said they did not think the

United States would have to fight Germany in their lifetime (AIPO). Thus, between April 1937 and 1938, more than half of the respondents believed that Germany was no more guilty than any other nation of causing World War I, 30 percent thought that the peace treaty was too severe, and over half believed that the United States would not have to fight Germany in their lifetime.

But significant changes occurred in the attitudes of the American public after the German annexation of the Sudeten area of Czechoslovakia. For example, when asked in October 1938 whether Germany's demand for the annexation of the Sudetenland in Czechoslovakia was justified, 77 percent answered "no" (AIPO). In August 1939, when the same question was asked about Germany's claims to the port of Danzig and the Polish corridor, 87 percent said they did not think these claims were justified (AIPO).

In response to news of a "peace pact" between Hitler and British Prime Minister Neville Chamberlain, that was arrived at during the Munich Conference, 60 percent said they thought that the pact would lead to a greater possibility of war

> Do you think that this settlement (Munich Agreement) will result in peace for a number of years or in a greater possibility of war (AIPO)?

Nevertheless at the same time, when asked whether they thought that England and France did the best thing in giving in to Germany instead of going to war, 59 percent answered "yes" (AIPO). One wonders whether the British and French publics, if asked these questions in the fall of 1938, might not have made the same responses. It was after the Munich Agreement that Neville Chamberlain, upon his return to London, told the press and the crowd awaiting him at the airport that there would be "peace in our time." The British and French publics might also have believed that it was the most practical alternative. It was better than going to war immediately, but it might increase the possibility of war at a later date.

After the conquest of Czechoslovakia and Hitler's announcement that he had no more territorial ambitions in Europe, the American public was asked whether or not it believed him; 92 percent said "no" (AIPO). A month before the invasion of Poland, when the public was asked whether it would like to see England, France, and Poland agree to German demands regarding Danzig,

88 percent said "no" (AIPO). The next month, after England and France honored their commitment and declared war on Germany following Germany's invasion of Poland, 82 percent said Germany was the country they considered responsible for causing the present war (AIPO). No other country was mentioned by more than 3 percent of the respondents.

Additional insight into the American public's attitudes toward Germany, once the European war had actually begun, is provided in their responses to the items of Table VI-5. Two months before

Table VI-5. Attitude toward Germany after European War Was Under Way, 1939–1941 (AIPO and FOR)

Item	Response	
1. Hitler says that the Polish question is settled and England and France have no reason to continue the war with Germany. Do you agree (AIPO)?	No	*October 1939* 86%
2. If England and France defeat Germany, should the peace treaty be _____ than at the end of the last war (AIPO)?	More severe Less severe Same	*December 1939* 58% 36 6
3. If it is clear that the Allies are beating Germany, do you think they should stop if Germany asks for peace, or do you think they should continue until Germany is so badly beaten that it will never again rise as a nation (FOR)?	Continue Stop Don't know	*January 1940* 57% 33 10

4. If Hitler offers to make peace this spring, do you think England and France should meet with Germany and try to end the war (AIPO)?		*March 1940*	*April 1941**
	Yes	75%	16%

5. If peace could be reached by letting Germany keep _____, would you be opposed (AIPO)?		*Yes*
	Czechoslovakia (March 1940)	62%
	Poland (November 1940)	70
	Countries it has (June 1941)	62
	Territory won from Russia (August 1941)	58

*In April 1941, only England was involved, since this was after the fall of France.

the defeat of France, in March 1940, 75 percent believed that it be desirable to work out a peace treaty if Hitler offered to do so. Presumably, given the response to Item 5 in Table VI–5 in which 62 and 70 percent were opposed to a deal that would permit Hitler to retain Czechoslovakia or Poland, such a treaty would involve relinquishing those territories. But a year later, only 16 percent believed that Britain should try to make peace rather than go on fighting. This difference between 75 and 16 percent is one index of the change in the public's beliefs about Germany's desire for peace and reflects a hardening of American attitudes toward Germany. But as late as November 1940, which was after the fall of France and the Low Countries, 54 percent advocated "doing business" (commercial business, that is) with Hitler, as witnessed by the fact that 54 percent chose the first alternative in the following item:

> If Hitler wins, should we find some way of continuing our European commercial business with Hitler's new Europe, or should we make every effort to develop business only with countries not under Hitler's control (AIPO)?

So much for Britain, France, and Germany. We turn next to a brief look at public opinion concerning the Soviet Union and the role it was likely to play in the European conflict. Between the mid-1930's and the summer of 1939, the United States perceived the Soviet Union as a potential ally against Germany should a world war develop. In August 1939, however, the Soviet Union and Germany signed a nonaggression pact, which provided that neither power would attack the other and that if one of them became the object of belligerent action by a third power, the other party would in no manner lend its support to this third power. The pact prepared the way for the German invasion of Poland and the subsequent absorption of Poland by Germany and Russia. The pact was broken when Hitler directed the German army to attack the Soviet Union in June 1941. Great Britain and the Soviet Union thus became allies.

In January 1939, seven months before the Hitler-Stalin pact was signed, and again in July 1941, one month after the pact was broken by Germany's invasion of the Soviet Union, the public was asked which side, Germany or Russia, it would rather see win. Both times there was practically no support for Germany (less than 5 percent); over 70 percent favored the Soviet Union. Most of the others said it made no difference or had no opinion. Public feeling about the Soviet Union, in the specific context of the lesser of two evils, had changed relatively little as a result of the pact. At about the same time, however, that the public indicated its preference for the Soviet Union, it also expressed the sentiments shown in Table VI-6 about the governments of the two nations. The question read:

> Which of the following statements most closely describes your feelings about the Russian and German governments (FOR)?

Table VI-6. Appraisal of Russian versus German Government, 1941 (FOR)

Statement	Agreement Percentage
1. The Russian government is worse than the German government.	5%
2. They are equally bad.	35
3. While there is not much choice between the two, the Russian government is slightly better.	32
4. The Russian government is far better than the German government.	8
5. Don't know	20

The responses in Table VI-6 were elicited in December 1941. They indicate that among the 80 percent who expressed an opinion, almost half believed that the Russian and German governments were equally bad. The other half believed that the Soviet government was "slightly better" or "far better" than the German.

We conclude this section on the public's opinion about its potential allies and enemies in World War II with a brief look at China and Japan. The earliest national polls that contained items about Japan's military activities appeared in the fall of 1937. By then, Japan and China had been at war for five years and Japan had occupied Manchuria since 1931. When asked in September 1937 with which side they sympathized, China or Japan, 55 percent answered "neither," 43 percent said "China," and 2 percent said "Japan." By June 1939, the trend shifted significantly in the direction of more sympathy for China. The results are shown in Table VI-7.

Table VI-7.   Sympathy with China versus
Japan, 1937-1939 (AIPO)

Month and Year	Neither	China	Japan
September 1937	55%	43%	2%
October 1938	40	59	1
June 1939	24	74	2

Table VI-8.   Trade with Japan, 1937-1940 (AIPO)

Item	Affirmative Percentage	
1. Is your sympathy for China great enough to keep you from buying goods made in Japan?	*October 1937* 37%	*June 1939* 66%
2. At the end of six months, when the trade treaty expires, should the United States refuse to sell Japan any more war materials?	*August 1939* 82%	
3. President Roosevelt has forbidden the shipment of scrap iron from this country to Japan. Do you approve?*	*October 1940* 96%	
4. Do you think our government should forbid the sale of arms, airplanes, gasoline, and other war materials to Japan?	*October 1940* 90%	

*The United States placed an embargo on the sale of scrap iron and steel to Japan in September 1940, after the Japanese army invaded French Indochina.

The same shifts in opinion may be observed in response to the items that comprise Table VI-8. Responses to all of the items in Table VI-8 indicate that the American public was almost unanimous in its willingness to support economic sanctions against Japan. Opinion, however, was more divided concerning diplomatic sanctions or military intervention. In the year preceding Pearl Harbor, when asked on three occasions, "Do you think the time has come for us to take strong measures against Japan?" the positive responses ranged from 49 to 69 percent (FOR). Even as late as December 1941, days before the attack on Pearl Harbor, the prospect of a confrontation with Japan was perceived by at least a third of the public as undesirable and to be avoided if possible.

Perhaps a more revealing measure of the public's reactions to Japanese activities in the Pacific may be seen in its responses to the following item, that appeared in October 1941:

> Which one of these statements comes closest to express-
> ing your feelings about Japan (AIPO)?

**Table VI-9. Attitude toward Japan before Pearl Harbor,
1941 (AIPO)**

Statement	Agreement Percentage
1. Japan has proved her right to grow, and we should not interfere with her.	4%
2. While Japan may be a threat in the future, we should not get excited about her until she attacks some of our territories or interferes with our supplies.	43
3. Japan has already gone far enough, and we should place our feet across her path and tell her another step means war.	34
4. Japan has already gone too far, and we should immediately declare war on her.	3
5. Don't know	16

Responses are shown in Table VI-9. Note that 43 percent advocated
a wait-and-see policy and did not anticipate having to take any
direct action against Japan in the immediate future; 16 percent felt
they did not know enough to voice an opinion. How long the public
would have been willing to maintain a wait-and-see attitude or
would have had no opinion became moot on December 7, 1941.

DURING WORLD WAR II

Duration of War and Outcome

When immediately following the United States' entry into the war,
the public was asked how long the war was likely to last, the modal
response (made by 38 percent) was "between two and five years."
Graph VI-3 describes expectations concerning the length of the
war made between January 1942 and January 1945.

In February 1944, five months after British and American
soldiers had landed in Italy, almost all of the respondents who were
willing to express an opinion thought the war in Europe would last
up to two more years, in Asia up to three more years. Between the

VI-3.   **Percent Saying War Would Last Various Lengths of Time, 1942–1944 (FOR)**

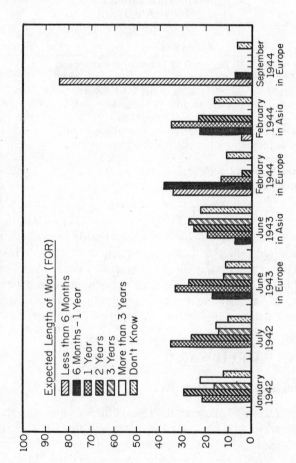

time the United States entered the war and the middle of 1943, there was relatively little shift in opinion. As of June 1943, almost as many people thought the war in Europe would be over in a year as thought it would go on for more than three years. But in February 1944, one third thought the war in Europe would be over in less than six months and 72 percent believed a year at the most. Note that twice as many respondents refused to make an estimate about the war in Asia. In September 1944, three months after the invasion of Normandy, 84 percent thought the war in Europe would be over within six months. The Battle of the Bulge in Germany had not yet begun, and the public, like many military experts, was basing its estimates on how quickly the Allied armies had progressed thus far. Concerning the war in Asia, in February 1944 only about one third as many thought the war in Asia would be over within a year (72 versus 26 percent). The modal response (made by 35 percent) was "between one and two years."

From the outset—that is, from December 1941—belief was widespread, although not unanimous, that the Allies would win the war, as witness the distribution of responses to the following item:

> Taking everything into consideration, which side do you think will win the war (FOR)?

The percentages were: Allies, 73%; Axis, 7%; Neither, 4%; Don't know, 16%.

Allies and Enemies

Until the fall of 1943, Germany was perceived as the country to beat. After September 1943 Japan became the Number 1 enemy, as shown in Table VI-10.

Table VI-10. Major Enemy—Germany or Japan, 1941-1944 (FOR)

Month and Year	Germany	Japan	Equal	Don't Know
December 1941	64%	15	21	—
June 1942	50	27	23	—
September 1943	25	57	12	6
August 1944	30	52	12	6

Throughout the war years, the American public was ambivalent about its alliance with the Soviet Union. The ambivalence was manifest in responses to items that probed how trustworthy the Soviet Union would be as an ally, how much support should be given to the Russians, and how likely it was that the United States and the Soviet Union would be able to work together after the war. Two months before and two months after the United States entered the war, the public was asked:

> Regardless of how you feel toward Russia, which of these policies do you think we should pursue toward her (FOR)?

Table VI-11.   Policy toward Soviet Union, 1941-1942 (FOR)

Statement	October 1941	February 1942
1. Stop helping Russia in any way.	14%	4%
2. Work along with Russia and give her some aid if we think it will help beat the Axis.	51	43
3. Treat Russia as a full partner along with Britain.	22	42
4. Don't know	13	11

Responses are given in Table VI-11. In February 1942, when the United States was on the defensive against the Japanese in the Pacific and the Soviet Union was bearing the major burden of the fighting in Europe, only 41 percent believed that Russia should be treated as a full partner. We note, however, that this figure represents an increase of 100 percent from the prewar attitudes reported in October 1941.

Table VI-12.   Cooperation of Soviet Union after the War, 1942-1945 (AIPO)

Month and Year	Yes	No	Undecided
March 1942	39%	39%	22%
April 1943	44	34	22
July 1944	47	36	17
December 1944	47	35	18
March 1945	55	31	14
June 1945	45	38	17
September 1945	54	30	16

When asked whether it thought Russia could be trusted to cooperate with us when the war was over, the American public was never strongly optimistic, as witness the distribution of responses reported in Table VI-12. Even with an increase of almost 50 percent, between March 1942 and September 1945, the percentage who believed Russia could be trusted did not exceed 55. The proportion who said they were undecided remained high throughout the war.

Perhaps even more revealing of the reservations the public had concerning the trustworthiness of the Soviet Union in the postwar era may be seen in its responses to the items in Table VI-13, asked between June and September 1943. The public did not perceive the Soviet Union to be as stable an ally as Britain or China. Almost 50 percent believed that Russia would make demands at the peace conference that the United States could not go along with, and over 40 percent anticipated that Russia would try to establish communist

Table VI-13. Expectations of Soviet Union after the War, 1943 (FOR and AIPO)

Item	*Response*			
1. Do you expect that Russia will want the same kind of peace that we do or that she will make demands that we can't agree to (FOR)?	Same kind of peace	30%		
	Demands we can't agree to	48		
	Don't know	22		
2. After the war, do you think Russia will or will not try to bring about Communist governments in other European countries (FOR)?	Will	41%		
	Will not	31		
	Don't know	28		
3. After the war, should the United States and Great Britain (U.S.S.R.) (China) make a permanent military alliance that the United States and Great Britain (U.S.S.R.) (China) agree to come to each other's defense immediately if the other is attacked at any future time (AIPO)?		*Great Britain*	*U.S.S.R.*	*China*
	Yes	61%	39%	56%
	No	25	37	23
	Undecided	14	24	21

regimes in the postwar governments of Europe. On each item there were over 20 percent who said they did not know or were undecided.

But even with the reservations expressed in the responses in Table VI-13, shortly after the war in Europe was over 75 percent believed that relations between the two countries would be either better in the future than they had been in the past or the same, but not worse. Table VI-14 gives the responses to the question:

> Thinking back for a moment to our relations with Russia (England) a few years before the war, do you think that we shall get along better with Russia in the future than we did in the past, not so well, or about the same (FOR)?

Table VI-14.   Future Relations with Soviet Union and England, 1945 (FOR)

Country	Better	Not as Good	About the Same	Don't Know
Soviet Union	48%	22%	20%	10%
England	31	19	44	6

American attitudes toward the Soviet Union are reviewed again in the next section on the postwar era. Now we report attitudes toward Germany and Japan during the war years, focusing primarily on the public's beliefs about how the defeated nations ought to be treated after the war. On the matter of the conditions under which the Allies should stop fighting, in the fall of 1943 the public was asked:

> Suppose the German army gets rid of Hitler, gives up all the territories Germany has conquered, and offers to make peace. If that happens, we should _____ (OPOR).

The responses were: Make peace if German army gives up conquered lands, 24%; Continue fighting until German army is crushed, 70%; Undecided, 6%.

In January 1944, 20 percent said they favored destroying Germany as a country after the war (AIPO). A month before the invasion of Normandy, 82 percent agreed that we should demand an unconditional surrender from Germany before we stop fighting (AIPO). When the same item was asked about Japan, two months before V.J. Day, and thus before atomic bombs were dropped on Hiroshima and Nagasaki, 84 percent said they favored an unconditional surrender from Japan (AIPO).

Public approval for unconditional surrender was related to its beliefs about how knowledgeable and responsible the German public was for the atrocities committed by Germany before and during the war. Pictures and statistics about the number of persons imprisoned and killed in concentration camps began to filter out to the American public after the Allied invasion of Western Europe in the summer of 1944. Public reactions to such information may be observed by their responses to the items in Table VI-15. From the estimates made to

Table VI-15.   German Atrocities, 1944–1945 (AIPO)

Item		Response	
1. Do you believe the stories that the Germans have murdered many people in concentration camps are true or not?		*December 1944*	*May 1945*
	True	76%	84%
	Exaggerated	—	9
	Not true	12	3
	No opinion	12	4
2. Nobody knows, of course, how many people have been murdered, but what would be your best guess?*		*December 1944* 100,000 or less (modal response) 35%	
		May 1945 1,000,000 or less (median response)	
3. Do you think it would be a good idea or a bad idea to have movie theaters throughout the country show pictures of all the horrible things that happened in prison camps run by Germans?			*May 1945*
	Good idea		60%
	Bad idea		35
	Undecided		5

*This question was asked of those who answered "true" to Item 1.

Item 2, it is reasonable to assume that the 60 percent who thought it would be a good idea to show the pictures did not realize the enormity of the atrocities that were committed. Official statistics mention figures above the 10,000,000 mark.

The public's relative innocence concerning the magnitude of the terror of the Nazi regime is also reflected in its responses to the following item (asked in June 1945), especially when responses, shown in Table VI–16, about Germany are compared with those about Japan:

> To what extent do you think the German people have approved of the killing and starving of prisoners in Germany (Japan) (AIPO)?

Table VI–16. Extent of German and Japanese Approval of Treatment of Prisoners, 1945 (AIPO)

People	Entire	Partial	None	Had No Knowledge	No Opinion
Germans	31%	51%	4%	8%	6%
Japanese	63	25	2	4	6

Twice as many were willing to believe that the Japanese people, as opposed to the Germans, would support fully a regime that practiced mass genocide and organized terror. It should be remembered, however, that in the early years of the war, much more publicity was given to the treatment of American prisoners of war by the Japanese after the defeats at Bataan, Corregidor, and other Pacific Islands and of the "long marches" to prison camps than to the treatment of prisoners by the Germans. By November 1945, when the Nazi treatment of Jews, Poles, Gypsies, and other groups was extensively publicized, Americans assessed the relative responsibility somewhat differently, as witness their responses, in Table VI–17, to the following question:

> Do you think many, only a few, or practically none of the civilian population in Japan (Germany) knew about the atrocities in prison camps while the war was still going on (FOR)?

Table VI–17. Extent of German and Japanese Knowledge of Treatment of Prisoners, 1945 (FOR)

People	Many	Few	Almost None	Don't Know
Germans	48%	38%	4%	10%
Japanese	37	45	6	12

Not only are the percentages closer together between the two countries, but there was a shift in direction, such that a higher proportion believed that many Germans knew as compared to Japanese.

Some indications of the extent of the anti-Japanese feeling prevalent in this country during the early years of the war are shown by responses to the items in Table VI-18, asked one year after Pearl

Table VI-18. Treatment of Japanese in United States after the War, 1942 (AIPO and NORC)

Item	Response	
1. Do you think the Japanese who were moved from the Pacific Coast should be allowed to return to the Pacific Coast when the war is over (AIPO)?*	All	35%
	Only citizens	26
	None	17
	Undecided	22
2. Would you be willing to hire Japanese servants to work in your home after the war is over (AIPO)?†	Yes	26%
	No	69
	Undecided	5
3. After the war, do you think the Japanese living in the United States should have as good a chance as white people to get any kind of job (NORC)?	Yes	16%
	Yes if loyal citizens	21
	No	61
	Undecided	2

*Under Article 7 of the Enemy Aliens Act, persons deemed dangerous to the public peace or safety of the United States were subject to summary apprehension. Enemy aliens were subject to confinement in such places of detention as was specified by the officers responsible for the execution of these regulations. The law was enforced almost exclusively against Japanese living in the United States.

†This question was asked of West Coast residents.

Harbor. It is interesting that none of these items was directed at persons living in the United States who emigrated from Germany or whose parents came from Germany. That fact in itself, perhaps more than the substantive responses, indicates stronger negative feelings toward the Japanese than toward the Germans.[1]

During World War II, a sentiment commonly expressed by Allied leaders, and one that was quickly adopted by the news commentators, was that we had won World War I on the battlefield but then lost the peace. The decision that nothing less than unconditional surrender would be acceptable from the Axis nations was one manifestation of the Allied leaders' desire not to make the same

[1] Of course, the item about the return of persons evacuated from the Pacific Coast would not apply to the Germans. But then, the fact that persons of Japanese background were evacuated and Germans were not is also evidence of the greater suspicion and animosity that were directed against the Japanese.

mistake again. Other manifestations of the serious consideration that the postwar period was receiving were the discussions concerning the extent and nature of the occupation by Allied forces of the defeated nations and the type of restructuring the Allies anticipated would be needed of the German and Japanese societies. Expressions of public opinion on this issue were obtained on several occasions during the war. For example, when asked what should be done with Germany and Japan as nations after the war, the public responded as shown in Table VI-19. The lack of similarity among

Table VI-19.   Disposition of Germany and Japan after the War, 1943-1945 (AIPO)

Month and Year	Super- vise Strictly	Destroy as Political Entity	Kill All	Reeducate and Rehabilitate	Miscel- laneous	No Opinion
November 1943 (Germany)	49%	21%	*	19%	—	11%
December 1944 (Japan)	28	33	13	8	18	—
May 1945 (Germany)	46†	34	*‡	8	—	12
August 1945§ (Japan)	53	*	14	33	3	7

*This choice was not given.
†The response included "punish war criminals."
‡The alternative response was "treat with extreme harshness."
§The percentages for August 1945 total 110% because some persons gave more than one answer.

the choices in the different surveys makes it somewhat difficult to compare attitudes toward the two nations, but there is enough comparability for us to conclude that the American public was committed to a policy of supervision and control for both.[2] A reflection of the public's greater animosity toward Japan than to Germany may be seen in the fact that 14 percent said they thought

[2] When asked about their reactions to the war crimes trials at Nuremberg (of which 87 percent said they had heard), 50 percent said they thought the court's verdicts were just about right and 39 percent thought the verdicts were too lenient. Only 4 percent believed they were too severe, and less than 7 percent had no opinion (AIPO).

all Japanese should be killed, but none considered that alternative as a solution to the German problem.

AFTER WORLD WAR II

Role in International Arena

The United States emerged from World War II as the major Western power. Twenty-one years earlier the United States had participated in a European conflict and had emerged then as an important world power. But both the United States Senate and Warren Harding, who succeeded Woodrow Wilson to the Presidency, opted for United States withdrawal from significant involvements in international affairs. The United States did not even join the League of Nations. During the two decades between the first and the second world war, the American public expressed misgivings at having allowed itself to be drawn into a conflict about which it basically had no interest and for which it received relatively little in the way of expressions of gratitude from nations with whom it had formed alliances. Isolationism became an attractive and comparatively simple policy for the President and others involved in shaping foreign policy to pursue. In this section, we trace the changes in the public's opinion concerning the role the United States ought to play in international politics, as well as its feelings about American involvement in World War II.

How dramatic the shift was, from an isolationist position to one that recognized the necessity of American involvement in world affairs, is shown most readily by responses to the following items:

1. Do you think the United States should join a world organization with police power to maintain world peace (AIPO)?

2. Do you think it would be best for the future of this country if we take an active part in world affairs (AIPO)?

Responses to the two questions are shown in Graph VI-4 and Table VI-20, respectively. Item 1 shows that between 1937 and 1945 there was an increase of over 300 percent in the proportion of respondents

VI-4. Percent Saying United States Should Join World Organization, 1937-1945 (AIPO)

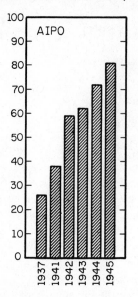

Table VI-20. United States Role in World Affairs, 1943-1951 (AIPO)

Month and Year	Active	Passive	No Opinion
March 1943	76%	14%	10%
May 1944	73	18	9
December 1945	71	19	10
October 1947	65	26	9
November 1948	62	30	8
March 1951	66	25	9

who favored the United States' joining a world organization.[3] Item 2 shows that the public's commitment to active participation in international affairs remained relatively stable after the shooting had subsided. It did wane somewhat during the worst phase of the cold war—that is, the period after the adoption of the Truman Doctrine, which involved promises of military aid to noncommunist regimes in Europe, and after Truman's victory in 1948.

[3]The United Nations Charter was drawn up at the San Francisco Conference in April 1945 and was attended by delegates from 46 nations.

In July 1945, a month before the war in the Pacific was over, the public was asked which country it thought would have the most influence in world affairs after the war. In response, 63 percent said the United States, compared to 24 percent who said the Soviet Union (AIPO). Unlike the situation vis-à-vis the League of Nations —plans for which the United States, in the person of President Wilson, initially formulated and supported and then refused to join—official as well as popular sentiment consistently supported the United Nations Organization and the United States never seriously considered withdrawing from it.

Between 1947 and 1957, when the public was asked, "Are you in favor of the United Nations Organization?" over 75 percent said "yes" (AIPO). Between 1947 and 1961, when asked on three occasions how important it was that the United States try to make the United Nations a success, between 79 and 82 percent answered "very important" (AIPO). In 1967, less than 15 percent said they thought the United States should give up its membership in the United Nations.[4] In 1970, 84 percent said they would like to see the United Nations become a stronger organization (AIPO).

Related to public beliefs expressed shortly after the end of the war that the United States should actively participate in international affairs and to the public's image of the United States as the major world power are the views that the public held concerning the rightness of American intervention in World War II. Almost twenty years after World War I was over, serious doubts were voiced about whether the United States should have participated in that war. Earlier we reported that in 1937, 60 percent thought it a mistake for the United States to have entered World War I. By 1941, the proportion dropped, but even then almost as many respondents said they thought it was a mistake as thought it was not (39 versus 42 percent). When the public was asked about the advisability of United States involvement in another war "like the world war," the percentages that advocated or favored such a venture ranged from 21 percent, in October 1941, to 17 percent, in March 1939 (AIPO).

The distribution of responses in Table VI-21 describes public

---

[4]Between 1953 and 1966, items appeared on national surveys that asked whether the United States should stay in or get out of the United Nations if Communist China was admitted. The percentage who said "get out" ranged from 25 to 5 percent. The lower proportions were given in the 1960's.

opinion toward American involvement in World War II within three years after the war was over. The question read:

Do you think it was a mistake for the United States to enter World War II (AIPO)?

Table VI-21. United States Entry in World War II a Mistake, 1946-1948 (AIPO)

Year	Yes	No	No Opinion
1946	15%	77%	8%
1947	24	66	10
1948*	17	78	5

*In 1948, the question read: "Now that the war has been over for three years and we've had a chance to think about the whole thing, how do you feel about our part in it? Do you think we had to get into the war in order to keep this country as you want it, or do you think it would have been better if we had kept out of the war entirely and let the rest of the world fight it?"

Unfortunately, there are no national poll data that describe the public's reactions to American involvement in World War I in the two or three years immediately following that war, and we have found no items that asked the public to reassess its opinion about American involvement in World War II two decades later. Thus, while the two sets of figures (reactions to United States involvement in the first and second world wars) are interesting and worth noting, they are not comparable. It is quite likely that with the passage of time a greater proportion would have come to believe that American involvement in World War II was a mistake also, especially during periods of tension between the United States and the Soviet Union or as trouble spots developed in different parts of the world.

Relations with the Soviet Union

How significant and how successful the United States would be in her new role as a major world power would depend in large measure on her ability to deal effectively with her wartime ally, the Soviet Union. Like the United States, the Soviet Union was also a relative neophyte cast in the role of star performer in the theater of international politics. With the defeat of Germany and Japan, and with the weakened position of Britain and France, the Soviet Union and the United States emerged as the two most important and powerful nations in the postwar world. The major advantages that the United States held were its virtual monopoly on atomic weapons and the fact that its countryside and economy had not been decimated by the war.

Earlier we reported that after V.E. Day twice as many respondents expected relations with the Soviet Union to be better than they had been in the past. We also indicated that 54 percent said they thought Russia could be trusted to cooperate with us when the war was over. In April 1946, British Prime Minister Winston Churchill made a foreign-policy speech in Fulton, Missouri, advocating in essence that Britain and the United States jointly adopt a hard-line policy toward their wartime ally. In a poll taken afterward, 68 percent of the persons asked said they had heard or read about Churchill's speech (AIPO). Of them, 60 percent said they disapproved of Churchill's suggestion that the United States and Great Britain form a military alliance as a check on the Soviet Union, 26 percent said they approved, 6 percent believed the United States and Britain should stick together but have no military alliance, and 8 percent had no opinion.

In the spring of 1946, a national poll carried the following item:

Do you think Russia will cooperate with us in world affairs (AIPO)?

Table VI-22. Cooperation of Soviet Union, 1946–1949 (AIPO)

Month and Year	Yes	No	No Opinion
March 1946	35%	52%	13%
January 1947	43	40	17
June 1949	20	62	18

The item appeared again in January 1947 and June 1949; the results are shown in Table VI-22. Even though 60 percent said they disapproved of Churchill's proposal for a joint military alliance against the Soviet Union, most respondents did not expect cooperation from the Soviet Union now that the war was over. By June 1949, which was six months after Truman had been elected to the Presidency and during which he had campaigned in favor of a harder line toward the Russians than some of the Roosevelt Democrats, notably Henry Wallace, had advocated, the proportion who expected cooperation from Russia dropped from 43 to 20 percent.

As early as 1946, which was one year after the war was over, 71 percent said that they disapproved of the policy Russia was following in world affairs (AIPO). Most people thought that the proper response to Russian behavior, as shown by their selection of the choices in Table VI-23, was to pursue a policy of firmness and to maintain a show of military strength.

Table VI-23.   Policy toward Soviet Union, 1946-1948 (AIPO)

Statement	1946	1948
1. Be firm—make her stick to agreements—no appeasement.	28%	22%
2. Keep strong—militarily prepared.	28	27
3. Go to war.	*	17
4. Go before the United Nations.	4	1
5. Get together and work things out.	4	2
6. Other	6	—
7. Do nothing—let her go—avoid trouble.	10	5
8. Miscellaneous / No opinion	20	26

*In 1946, this choice was not given.

"Go to war" was not included in the response categories in 1946, but it is not unlikely, given the similarity of responses to the first two alternatives that as many as 17 percent might not have selected that choice, even as early as 1946. The fact that hardly anyone chose the United Nations alternative may reflect knowledge of the existence of the veto power held by each of the major powers, and therefore the futility of such action. Much the same range of opinions was manifest in response to the following item, that was included in a 1946 poll:

> Which of these statements comes closest to stating what you believe is the best way to deal with Russia in order to make peace (FOR)?

Responses are shown in Table VI-24. By the fall of 1946, when the public was asked whether its feelings toward Russia were more or less friendly than they were a year ago 62 percent said "less" (AIPO).

Table VI-24. Posture vis-à-vis Soviet Union to Preserve Peace, 1946 (FOR)

Statement	Agreement Percentage
1. Russia will cooperate with us to maintain peace if we try to understand her point of view and make some concessions in order to help solve her immediate problems.	24%
2. Russia won't cooperate with us as long as we give in to her. The best way to get her to work with us for peace is to keep strong ourselves and make concessions only when we get something in return.	62
3. Don't know	14

A year later, most of the public shared at least two feelings about the Soviet Union and the quality of the relationship the United States ought to maintain with her. The first was that Russia

Table VI-25. Soviet Union's Aggressiveness and Expansionism, 1945-1949 (FOR and AIPO)

Item		Response	
1. Would you describe Russia as a peace-loving nation, willing to fight only if she has to defend herself, or as an aggressive nation that would start a war to get something she wants (FOR)?		*September 1945*	*October 1947*
	Peace-loving	39%	12%
	Aggressive	38	66
	Both*	8	6
	No opinion	15	16

Item		*July 1946*	*October 1947*	*March 1948*	*June 1949*
2. As you hear and read about Russia these days, do you believe Russia is trying to build herself up to be the ruling power of the world, or is Russia just building up protection against being attacked in another war (AIPO)?	Ruling power	58%	76%	77%	66%
	Protection	29	18	12	15
	No opinion	13	6	11	19

*Respondents volunteered this response; it was not included among the choices.

had become a major threat to world peace. The second was that by setting up satellite governments in countries on her western and southern borders immediately following the end of the war, Russia demonstrated expansionist interests and designs on Western Europe and Asia. Both of these feelings are represented in the public's responses to the items in Table VI-25.

In 1946, 71 percent had said they disapproved of Russia's foreign policy (AIPO). By the fall of 1947, over 60 percent also disapproved of American policy vis-à-vis the Soviet Union. By a ratio of two and a half to one, most people believed the United States was being too soft on Russia. When the same item appeared on three later polls between October 1947 and Semptember 1949, the percentage who believed the United States was being too soft increased and then declined slightly, as shown in Table VI-26. The reduction

Table VI-26. Toughness of United States Policy toward Soviet Union, 1947-1949 (AIPO)

Month and Year	Too Soft	Too Tough	About Right	No Opinion
October 1947	62%	6%	24%	8%
March 1948	73	3	11	13
July 1948	69	6	14	11
September 1949*	53	10	26	11

*In 1949, the alternatives were slightly different: instead of "too soft," the choice read "should be even firmer"; and instead of "too tough," the choice was "should be more willing to compromise."

in the "too soft" category and the increase in the "about right" slot that occurred between the summer of 1948 and the fall of 1949 may have reflected public approval of the changes that had occurred in American policy, as represented by the Truman Doctrine and the stance the United States had assumed during the meetings of foreign ministers that were held in Europe in 1948 and 1949 on the unification of Germany and the Berlin situation.

> Do you think the United States is being too soft or too tough in its policy toward Russia (AIPO)?

An issue that does not seem particularly important today but which in the first decade following World War II had a sense of urgency and an almost magical quality attached to it, was the possibility of a summit meeting between the Russian and American heads of state. Whenever the temperature in the cold war dropped precipitously or some event occurred that altered the delicate balance in Soviet-American relations, the possibility was raised that the leaders of the two major powers would meet face to face and work things out. The American public always responded to the possibility of top-level talks with optimism. As the responses in Graph VI-5 indicate, it made little difference who the head of state of either country was, a face-to-face meeting was always viewed as a good idea.

VI-5. Percent Approving of Top-Level Talks, 1948–1961 (AIPO and NORC)

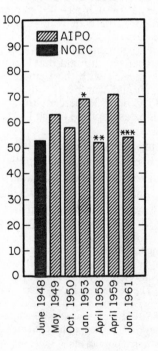

We conclude this section on American-Soviet relations in the postwar era by citing four sets of responses that describe in a general way the public's long-term expectations and hopes for the kind of relationship that might be worked out between the two major powers:

1. From 1948 to 1961, between 76 and 82 percent supported the government policy of maintaining troops in Berlin even though the Russians "make things difficult" (AIPO).
2. At the most, 64 percent in 1954 and at the least 40 percent in 1959 thought that there was bound to be a major war sooner or later with the Soviet Union (AIPO).[5]
3. The emergence of the Communist regime in China as a major power affected public opinion about Soviet-United States relations. In 1961, when asked which country would be the greater threat to world peace in 1970—Russia or China—49 percent said Russia, compared to 32 percent who said China. When the same question was asked in 1967, 69 percent said China and 20 percent Russia (AIPO).[6]
4. In 1967, 46 percent thought that Russia would be more likely to ally itself with the United States as opposed to China, should war break out between the United States and China; 36 percent thought Russia would choose China as opposed to the United States (AIPO).

The consistent theme that emerges from these responses is that the American public has advocated a policy of firmness, military preparedness, and recognition of Russia as a serious and potential danger. Another, and perhaps at the present time, minor theme in the public's assessment is the belief that in the long run the older, more industrialized, urbanized, and bureaucratized Soviet Union

[5] It is interesting to compare these responses with those given to the item that appeared in a 1938 survey about the likelihood of war between the United States and Nazi Germany. In 1938, 54 percent did *not* expect to have to fight Germany. The responses for 1959 may have reflected America's greater fear of the Soviet Union as opposed to the Nazi regime, or its greater conviction that the Soviet Union was more aggressive than Germany was. But most likely they reveal the public's greater sophistication about the intricacies of international politics and a sense of psychological preparedness. The American public evidently did not wish to perceive itself as the ostrich hiding its head in the sand, a posture it may have believed it had assumed a generation ago.

[6] In 1967, the question read "looking ahead to the next few years" for "in 1970."

would perceive itself as having more in common with a major affluent and bourgeois Western power than with militant and relatively youthful Communist governments that were still fervent with revolutionary zeal. Russia and the United States may both come to perceive themselves as reluctant partners who need each other to protect their accomplishments, their wealth, and their power against upstarts of various ideological persuasions.

Use and Control of Nuclear Bombs

The postwar era found the United States confronted with a new and awesome problem: how atomic power might be used for destructive as well as peaceful purposes. This section reviews the public's responses to the dropping of atomic bombs on the Japanese cities of Hiroshima and Nagasaki, proposals for collective control and supervision of atomic energy, the continued testing of atomic weapons, and the possibility of a nuclear war.

We look first at Americans' reactions to the dropping of atomic bombs on Hiroshima and Nagasaki. Within days after the bombs were dropped, the public was asked whether it approved or disapproved: 85 percent said they approved, 10 percent disapproved, and 5 percent had no opinion (AIPO). The small percentage of persons in the "no opinion" category is especially noteworthy in this context. Just a few days before, an event without precedent in the history of the world had occurred. For practically all Americans it must have come as a complete surprise. There could have been no preparation for absorbing the enormity of the act. Yet, only days after the event, when it is fair to assume that most people still did not understand the consequences of the act or indeed the factors that had been involved in the decision to use the bomb, only 5 percent said "no opinion."

Three months later, in November 1945, another item on the same topic appeared; responses are given in Table VI-27. We note

Which of these comes closest to describing how you feel about our use of the atomic bomb (FOR)?

that there was still widespread support for our having used the bomb. Indeed, there was a larger percentage who believed that we

Table VI–27.   United States Use of Atomic Bomb, 1945 (FOR)

Statement	Agreement Percentage
1. We should not have used any atomic bombs at all.	4%
2. We should have dropped one first on some upopulated region, to show the Japanese its power, and dropped the second one on a city if they hadn't surrendered after the first one.	14
3. We should have used the two bombs on the cities just as we did.	54
4. We should have quickly used many more of them before Japan had a chance to surrender	23
5. Don't know	5

should have used more of them than who opposed use at all or who felt we should have stopped after the first.

It is reasonable to assume that support for use of the atomic bomb and perceptions about how long the war in the Pacific was likely to last would be related. When the public was asked in November 1945 how much longer it thought the Japanese would have held out if it had not been for the atomic bomb, the distribution was as shown in Table VI–28. Over 50 percent believed that the war would have lasted more than six months longer if we had not used the bomb, and only 8 percent thought use of the bomb had no effect on the length of the war.

Table VI–28.   Duration of War If Not for Atomic Bomb, 1945 (FOR)

Duration	Agreement Percentage
No longer	8%
2–6 months	27
6–11 months	21
1 year	15
More than 1 year	18
Don't know	11

The next item asked how the public felt about the fact that such a bomb had been developed. Responses are shown in Table VI–29.

Do you think that it was a good thing or a bad thing that
the atomic bomb was developed (AIPO)?

**Table VI-29. Atomic Bomb—Good or Bad
Development, 1945-1949 (AIPO)**

Month and Year	Good	Bad	No Opinion
September 1945	69%	17%	14
February 1946*	47	18	15 (20)
October 1947	55	38	7
March 1949	59	27	14

*In 1946, the question read: "Do you think that the discovery
of the atomic bomb increases or decreases the possibility of
another war?" And the alternatives were: "decreases," which we
say is a proxy for "good"; "increases," "no difference," and "no
opinion." The figure in parentheses is the "no difference" percentage.

During this period (1945-1949) the United States was not involved
in a war, and thus there was no immediate issue concerning the
justness or legitimacy of using an atomic bomb. In this relatively
hypothetical context, at least one and a half times as many respondents believed it was a good thing that the bomb had been developed
as thought it a bad thing. The proportion of those who thought it
bad, however, increased over time, perhaps as a function of the
greater availability of information about the bomb's destructive
capabilities.

Less than a year and a half after the last survey which asked
whether it was good or bad that the bomb was developed, the
United States was involved in a war, and the issue became less
speculative. In the summer of 1950, President Truman accused the

**Table VI-30. Atomic-Bomb Use in Korea and in Another
World War, 1950 (AIPO)**

Item	Response	
1. Do you think the United States should or should not use the atomic bomb in Korea?	Should	28%
	Should not	60
	No opinion	12
2. What is your opinion about our using the atomic bomb if the United States got into another *world* war—do you think we should or should not use it?	Should	61 ⎫ 77%
	Qualified should	16 ⎬
	Should not	16 ⎭
	No opinion	7

North Koreans of crossing the 49th Parallel and thereby invading the territory of South Korea. American troops were sent to help in the defense of South Korea, and thus the United States was at war with North Korea. Shortly thereafter, the public was asked the items in Table VI-30. In their responses to both items, the American public made it clear that while it condoned the use of atomic weapons to defeat Japan and would support using the A-bomb in another major conflict, it did not wish to see atomic weapons used in "limited" wars or wars that did not involve the Soviet Union. While 60 percent opposed using atomic weapons in Korea, 61 percent unequivocally supported their use should a world war develop.

Within one month after the bombs exploded on Nagasaki and Hiroshima in August 1945, questions appeared on national polls about whether the United States should, or under what conditions would, share its knowledge of how to produce atomic bombs. The initial item read:

> Do you think the secret of making atomic bombs should be put under the control of the new United Nations Security Council, or should the United States keep this secret to itself (AIPO)?

In response, 71 percent favored having the United States keep the secret to itself (AIPO). During this initial period not only did the public favor secrecy on the matter of production, but most also opposed having foreign observers at testing sites or sharing information concerning the result of such tests: 66 percent answered both of the following questions in the negative:

> 1. This summer our navy plans to make tests at sea to find out how effective the atomic bombs would be in naval warfare. Do you think that representatives of other nations should or should not be allowed to watch these tests (AIPO)?
> 2. Do you approve of giving other nations a complete report of the results of the tests (AIPO)?

Indeed, when the American public was first given an opportunity to react to a major plank in the Baruch Plan, namely, the establishment of a system of international inspection, the proposal did not meet with widespread support.[7] The following question was asked in 1946 and again in 1968:

> It has been suggested that the world organization have inspectors who could search any property in any country at any time to see if anybody was making atomic bombs. All inspectors would work in teams, having one Russian, one Englishman, and one American working together. Do you think there should be such an inspection or not (NORC)?

Responses are given in Table VI-31. The lack of enthusiasm for inspection and for sharing atomic secrets was related to the pessimism that pervaded public opinion about the Soviet Union during this period (as witnessed by responses in the previous section), and to the widespread belief that the United States might be able to maintain its monopoly position.

Table VI-31. International Inspection for Atomic-Bomb Manufacture, 1946–1968 (NORC)

Month and Year	Favor	Oppose	Undecided
July 1946	39%	50%	11%
May 1968	43	39	18

As it became more and more apparent that the United States could not for long maintain a monopoly of the technical and scientific knowhow necessary to produce atomic weapons, the public became more responsive to plans that involved inspection and international control. For example, in January 1947, when asked the following question, 74 percent acknowledged that atomic weapons could not guarantee American invulnerability.

[7]The Baruch Plan, presented to the United Nations in June 1946, represented the United States position on control of the atomic bomb. The major provisions were that the manufacture of atomic bombs would stop, existing bombs would be disposed of, and an international commission would have full information concerning knowhow for the production of atomic stockpiles. These provisions were contingent upon the ratification of international agreements concerning the right of inspection by teams of "competent persons" representing many nations.

Do you think that the United States could become so strong by making atomic bombs and rockets that no other country will dare attack us, or do you think that regardless of how strong we become, someday another country might think she is stronger and attack us (NORC)?

The responses were: Another country might attack us, 74%; No country would dare attack us, 19%; Undecided, 7%.

When asked to choose between strengthening the United Nations even at the cost of infringing on the United States' own sovereignty, and building bigger, better, and more bombs, over twice as many opted for international discussion and control.

If the United States could do only one of these two things during the next few years, which one do you think would give us the best chance of keeping peace in the world? Should we try to make the United Nations organization strong enough to prevent all countries, including the United States, from making atomic bombs and rockets, or should we try to keep ahead of other countries by making more and better atomic bombs and rockets (NORC)?

The answers were: Make the United Nations strong, 67%; Try to keep ahead, 28%; Undecided, 5%.

By January 1948, 60 percent said they supported international control, as shown in Table VI–32, and 78 percent thought the United States ought to halt its production of atomic bombs even before an international control agency was established.

1. Which of these statements comes closest to summing up your opinion about international control of atomic energy (NORC)?
2. Do you believe that the United States should agree to stop making atomic bombs before an international control agency is set up (NORC)?

Within two years after these items appeared, the issue of international control and production of atomic bombs gave way to considerations of an even more destructive weapon, and one that has never been used: the hydrogen bomb. February 1950 was the first time a national survey asked about the H-bomb, and at that

Table VI–32.   International Control of Atomic Energy, 1948 (NORC)

Statement	Agreement Percentage
1. International control of atomic energy has a very good chance of working, and I think we should try it.	28%
2. International control of atomic energy has a fair chance of working, but I think we ought to try it.	32
3. International control has only a fair chance of working, and I don't think we ought to risk it.	15
4. International control can't possibly work, and there's no use trying it.	13
5. Undecided	12

time 70 percent of the American public said they had heard or read about it (AIPO). Of those, 49 percent believed that they were well enough informed to offer some arguments for or against its manu-facture, and 77 percent said they favored United States production of it. Two months later, a national survey questioned respondents again about whether they had heard or read about the hydrogen bomb; 85 percent answered that they had (AIPO). All respondents (those who said they had heard of the bomb and those who said they had not) were then given a brief description of the bomb which read as follows:

> It has been decided that the United States should try to make a hydrogen bomb which may be up to a thousand times *more powerful than the atom bomb*. What is your opinion of our going ahead and trying to make such a bomb (AIPO)?

The initial response, as shown in Table VI–33, concerning the advisability of manufacturing the hydrogen bomb was to support its development.

From the mid-1950's until 1963, the debate about atomic weapons focused on the issue of how a collective agreement could be reached that would prohibit above-ground nuclear tests. The issue was finally resolved in 1963 when the United States joined the Soviet Union and 100 other nations in signing a nuclear-test-ban treaty. Before the treaty, some variation of the following question appeared on national surveys at regular intervals:

Do you think the United States should stop making tests
with nuclear weapons and H-bombs (AIPO)?

Table VI-33.   Manufacture of Hydrogen Bomb, 1950 (AIPO)

Statement	Agreement Percentage
1. Approval: go ahead; we must be prepared.	69%
2. Qualified or reluctant approval: make it but don't use it; for defense only; if Russia has one; only as a last resort.	9
3. Disapproval: don't make it; never should be made.	14
4. No opinion	8

**Table VI-34.   United States Cessation of
Nuclear Tests, 1953-1958 (AIPO)**

Month and Year	Yes	No	No Opinion
April 1953	20%	71%	9%
October 1956	24	56	20
May 1958	29	60	11

As shown in Table VI-34, the public showed little enthusiasm for a
unilateral ban on nuclear testing during the 1950's. But by 1957 it
was willing to endorse a ban on nuclear tests and the production
of atomic weapons if there were assurances that the Soviet Union
would also refrain from tests and production. Table VI-35 gives the
distribution of responses. The public thus supported banning and
inspection, so long as these actions were accompanied by meaning-
ful assurances that the United States would be neither first nor alone
in taking such action.

Table VI-35.   Nuclear-Test Ban and Inspection, 1957 (AIPO)

Item	Response	
1. If all other nations, including Russia, agree to stop making any more tests with nuclear weapons and H-bombs, should the United States agree to stop or not?	Should Should not No opinion	63% 27 10
2. Would you favor or oppose setting up a worldwide organization which would make sure by regular inspection that no nation, including Russia and the United States, makes hydrogen bombs, atom bombs, and missiles?	Favor Oppose No opinion	70% 16 14

Foreign Aid

After World War II the United States entered the international loan and aid business on a scale never before engaged in by any country in the world. Given the isolationist leanings that were so deeply imbedded in the American political character from the birth of the nation through the period immediately preceding the onset of World War II, it is reasonable to expect that this new role the government was prepared to assume would have aroused at least ambivalent, if not strong negative, reactions among large portions of the American public. In this section, we trace attitudes toward foreign aid on a massive scale by concentrating on the period immediately following the end of the war.

In October 1945, two months after the end of the war, the items in Table VI-36 appeared on a national poll. Twice as many

Table VI-36. United States Loan to Soviet Union and England, 1945 (AIPO)

Item	Response	
1. Russia has asked this country for a loan of six billion dollars to help Russia get back on its feet. Would you approve or disapprove of the United States making such a loan?	Approve	27%
	Disapprove	60
	No opinion	13
2. England plans to ask this country for a loan of three to five billion dollars to help England get back on its feet. Would you approve or disapprove of the United States making such a loan?	Approve	27%
	Disapprove	60
	No opinion	13

people opposed rather than favored making the loan. But of even greater interest is the fact that the public responded to both nations in identical fashion.

In June 1947 Secretary of State George Marshall delivered a commencement address at Harvard in which he described a plan for the rehabilitation of Europe. That plan eventually became known as the European Recovery Act or the Marshall Plan. Its purpose was "the revival of a working economy in the world so as to permit the emergence of political and social conditions in which free institutions can exist" (Acheson, 1970, p. 311). Six months later, in December 1947, President Truman asked Congress to enact the Marshall

Plan. In his address to the Congress the President said (Bernstein and Matusow, 1966, p. 266):

> The people of the United States have shown, by generous contributions since the end of hostilities, their great sympathy and concern for the many millions in Europe who underwent the trials of war and enemy occupation. Our sympathy is undiminished, but we know that we cannot give relief indefinitely and so we seek practical measures which will eliminate Europe's need for further relief.
>
> Considered in terms of our own economy, European recovery is essential. The last two decades have taught us the bitter lesson that no economy, not even one so strong as our own, can remain healthy and prosperous in a world of poverty and want.

When the public was first given the opportunity to express its opinion of the plan, 57 percent said they approved of it (AIPO). Between July 1947 and May 1950, items referring specifically to the Marshall Plan were included on at least a dozen national polls and the proportions that indicated support for the program ranged between 50 and 60 percent.[8]

The Marshall Plan applied to the countries of Western Europe. In his inaugural address in January 1949, President Truman laid down four major guidelines for his foreign policy. The first two were support of the United Nations and endorsement of the European Recovery Act (Marshall Plan). Essentially these points were extensions of policies of the previous administration. The next two were new proposals. They involved strengthening the free nations against aggression by "providing unmistakable proof of the joint determination of the free countries to resist armed attack from any quarter" and a plan to "embark on a bold new program for making the benefits of our scientific advances and industrial progress available for the improvement and growth of underdeveloped areas" (Acheson, 1970, pp. 349-350). The last part, which became known as the Point Four Program, was directed primarily at the less developed countries of Asia, Africa, and Latin America. The

---

[8] Evidence that the plan had received considerable coverage in the mass media is shown by the fact that between July 1947 and November 1948, the proportion who said they had heard or read about it increased from 49 to 82 percent.

public's endorsement of Point Four is shown in its response, which appears in Table VI-37, to the following item:

> In general, do you think it is a good policy for the United States to try to help backward countries to raise their standard of living, or shouldn't this be any concern of our government (NORC)?

Table VI-37. United States Aid to Underdeveloped Nations, 1949–1950 (NORC)

Month and Year	Good Policy	Not Our Concern	Don't Know
March 1949	72%	23%	5%
November 1949	75	20	5
April 1950	73	22	5

In the years that followed the end of World War II, the American public exhibited a willingness to assume responsibilities for the well-being and protection of other nations that were qualitatively different and greater than any role the nation had played in the past. This new "largess" was probably influenced by a sense of self-interest, as witness responses to this item which appeared on a national survey in June 1950:

> Do you think such help to backward countries would really help the United States in any war or wouldn't it help us at all (NORC)?

The responses were: Would, 70%; Would not, 22%; Don't know, 8%.

By the late 1950's and early 1960's, some of the public's enthusiasm for massive foreign aid may have diminished. When appropriation bills were debated in Congress during the Eisenhower administration and the public was asked for its opinion, it responded as shown in Table VI-38. Unlike responses to the Point Four Program and other issues involving foreign aid, a greater proportion of the public did not have an opinion on the matter of appropriations. Among those who did, there seemed to be a tendency to select the affirmative choices without regard for the meaning of the item. Thus, note that a higher proportion thought that Congress should appropriate the same amount this year *and* that

Table VI-38.   Foreign-Aid Appropriations, 1956-1957 (AIPO)

Item		Response	
1. During recent years Congress has appropriated about four billion dollars each year for countries in other parts of the world to help prevent their going communistic. Should Congress appropriate the same amount this year or not?	Should Should not No opinion	*February 1956* 57% 25 18	*January 1957* 58% 28 14
2. Eisenhower says that there should not be a big cut in the United States aid to foreign countries. Some members of Congress say there should be. Do you, yourself, think there should or should not be a big cut in foreign aid?	Should Should not No opinion	*May 1957* 42% 32 26	

there should be a big cut in foreign aid. This phenomenon, known as the "acquiescence syndrome," tends to occur when respondents are not particularly interested in the items or do not fully understand their meaning. Probably on this matter, questions pertaining to appropriations involving millions of dollars were not topics about which the public felt competent to make informed opinions and therefore acquiesced to the direction implied by the choice of responses.

We conclude this section by noting responses to the issue of foreign aid when the question was phrased in the most general of terms and in a manner in which the public probably felt competent to respond:

> How do you feel about foreign aid—are you for or against it (AIPO)?

As shown in Table VI-39, in 1966, two decades after the end of World War II, one and a half times as many respondents favored a program of massive foreign aid as opposed it. Between 1958 and 1966, there was little shift in the distribution of responses on this issue. On this aspect of foreign policy, there are no significant signs

Table VI-39. General Attitude on Foreign Aid, 1958-1966 (AIPO)

Month and Year	Favor	Oppose	No Opinion
March 1958	51%	33%	16%
March 1963	58	30	12
April 1965	57	33	10
March 1966	53	35	12

that the American public is about to revert to the isolationism that had characterized it in the first half of the twentieth century. There might be times, however, when the United States will be less generous, depending probably on what the nation thinks it is getting in return and on the health of the American economy.

Relations with China

One of the major events of the postwar era was the demise of Chiang Kai-shek's Kuomintang regime in China and the assumption of power by the Communists. Among the more important international consequences that the Communist takeover had was to alter the political map of Asia, shift power relations within the communist camp, and influence a change in relations between the Soviet Union and the United States. Of all its relations with nations that have played significant roles in the arena of international politics, the American government's stance vis-à-vis the People's Republic of China has been the most monolithic. At the time of writing, the United States is the only major power to refuse official recognition of Mainland China. Until the 1971 session of the United Nations, it had consistently rallied forces to vote against seating the Mainland Chinese government as a member nation of that organization.

The discussion that is provided here, of the public's perception of Communist China, is focused primarily on the issue of American recognition of the Communist government and the acceptance of the Peking regime into the United Nations. In 1949, there were a few instances when the American public was asked about its attitudes toward the Chiang Kai-shek regime and what, if anything, the United States should do to bolster the Nationalist government. As the responses indicate, lack of knowledge and absence of opinion on the topics in question composed a large segment of the response pattern.

The items included in national polls in the summer and fall of 1949, just prior to the toppling of the Nationalist Chinese government, are provided in Table VI-40. The high proportion of "no opinions" and

Table VI-40.   Attitude toward China before Communist Takeover, 1949-1950 (AIPO)

Item	Response		
1. What is your opinion of Chiang Kai-shek?			*1949*
	Generally unfavorable		35%
	Generally favorable		21
	No opinion		44
2. Do you think the United States should or should not try to help Chiang Kai-shek?		*1949*	*1950*
	Should	25%	48%
	Should not	44	35
	No opinion	31	17
3. Is there anything the United States should do, in your opinion, to stop China from going communist?			*1949*
	Yes*		21%
	No		36
	Don't know		43
4. Do you think the communists will take over all of China?			*1949*
	Yes		48%
	No		23
	No opinion		29

*Send economic and military aid.

"don't know" responses to each item, is indicative of the relatively low order of interest or importance that China had for the American public. Among those who did have an opinion, there was not much interest in helping Chiang Kai-shek. More people were unfavorably disposed toward him than favorably disposed. This negative view of Chiang Kai-shek was probably formed after the war, when information appeared in the mass media about massive corruption within the Chinese government which Chiang Kai-shek apparently condoned and may even have benefited from directly.

Corruption on an extraordinarily wide scale was combined with the image that the Kuomintang government had little interest in or plans for bringing about major economic and social reforms, without which the country could not begin to overcome the vast damage done to its economy and social organization after more than a dozen years of war. In addition, other information that did much to lower the estimation of the former hero (and his wife) in the eyes of the American public was his failure to organize an effective fighting force against the Japanese, choosing instead to use his army (which was supplied mainly with American arms and equipment) to fight the Chinese communists. Publicity of this kind appeared in the American press only after the war had ended. It undoubtedly did much to lower American esteem for Chiang Kai-shek and to explain the public's lack of interest in preserving his government. It is interesting to note that while the public appeared to view the Chiang government as hopeless, the Congress, from V.J. Day through 1948, appropriated approximately a billion dollars in military aid and a similar amount in economic aid to the Nationalist government (Acheson, 1970, p. 400).

The American public and the government, however, shared a common perspective in their unwillingness to recognize the new People's Republic. In November 1949, months after Mao Tse-tung became premier, the public was asked:

> Do you think the United States should recognize the new government in China that is being set up by the Chinese Communist Party? That is, do you think we should send an ambassador and have dealings with this government in China (AIPO)?

Table VI-41.   United States Recognition of Communist China, 1949-1950 (AIPO)

Month and Year	Favor	Oppose	No Opinion	Unfamiliar
November 1949	20%	42%	14%	24%
June 1950	16	40	9	35

As Table VI-41 shows, of those with an opinion, more than twice as many opposed as favored recognition. But the combined percentage of those with no opinion and of those who were unfamiliar with the issue was as great as, or greater than, the percentage of those who opposed recognition on either occasion.

The two questions about China that were asked more often on national surveys than any others in the postwar period—and for many Americans may have come to characterize the essence of United States policy toward Peking—were whether Communist China should be admitted to the United Nations and whether it should replace Nationalist China on the Security Council. Responses to the first question are shown in Graph VI-6, and to the second question in Table VI-42. The major shift in opinion occurred in response to the first item about whether Communist China ought to be admitted to the United Nations. In 1954 only 7 percent advocated such a policy and 78 percent opposed China's admittance. By 1971, the situation had changed considerably, such that 45

VI-6.   Percent Favoring Admission of Communist China to United Nations, 1954-1971 (AIPO)

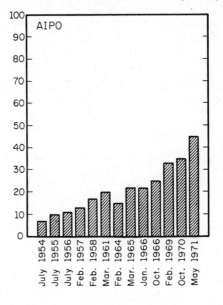

Table VI-42.   Replacement of Nationalist with Communist China on Security Council, 1950-1958 (AIPO)

Month and Year	Favor	Oppose	No Opinion
September 1950	11%	58%	31%
August 1954	8	79	13
June 1955	10	67	23
July 1956	11	74	15
February 1957	13	70	17
February 1958	17	66	17
September 1958	20	63	17

percent supported and 38 percent opposed. The responses reported in May 1971 occurred after the Peking government had invited the American Ping-Pong team to China but before President Nixon's announcement that he would visit China early in 1972.[9]

We conclude by noting the same two items that appeared in the last part of the section on American–Soviet relations, because the items and the responses made to them seem still to summarize the public's perceptions of the complicated relations that exist and that are likely to exist among the three major powers. Table VI–43 contains the items and the public's responses. The American public made these responses before the Ping-Pong invitation and before President Nixon's announcement of his planned visit, and at the time when attention was focused on the Middle East and the Soviet presence in that area. In 1967, Americans believed that in the long run the Soviet Union would feel more threatened by China than by the United States and that China would be the major power that would threaten world peace. The questions shown in Table VI–43 have not appeared on national polls since the 1967 Middle East crisis developed and since the Ping-Pong invitation and the planned visit were announced.

Table VI–43. United States Relations with Soviet Union and China, 1961–1967 (AIPO)

Item	Response		
		1961	*1967*
1. Looking ahead to 1970 (or the next few years), which country do you think will be the greater threat to world peace— Russia or China?	Russia	49%	20%
	China	32	69
	No opinion	19	11
			1967
2. If trouble ever broke out between the United States and China, do you think Russia would be more likely to be on our side or on China's side?	United States		46%
	China		36
	No opinion		18

[9]More evidence for the shift in opinion about willingness to admit Communist China to the United Nations is reflected in the public's response to this item that also appeared in a national survey in May 1971: "Suppose a majority of the members of the U.N. decide to admit Communist China to the U.N. Do you think the United States should go along with the U.N. decision or not (AIPO)?" In response, 58 percent said "yes," 28 percent said "no," and 14 percent said they didn't know.

THE KOREAN AND VIETNAM WARS

We cannot conclude this discussion of foreign policy without some references to public opinion concerning American involvement in Vietnam. Public opinion about the war in Vietnam has probably been reported more frequently and more exhaustively than about any previous war. The public's ultimate assessment of the government's policy of committing troops to Vietnam and of engaging in an undeclared war for over a decade cannot be determined while the conflict continues. We describe public sentiment toward the Vietnam War during a period in which government policy is still being determined and when public sentiments are in a state of flux. One strategy that we adopted for reporting opinion about Vietnam was to compare it against public attitudes toward the Korean War, which was the first long-term conflict since World War II in which American troops were actively involved.

A question with almost identical wording appeared on national polls in both the 1950's during the Korean War and again in the 1960's during the Vietnam conflict:

> In view of the developments since we entered the fighting in Korea (Vietnam), do you think the United States made a mistake in going into the war (in sending troops to fight) in Korea (Vietnam) (AIPO)?

The pattern of responses as shown in Graph VI-7, is remarkably similar. At the outset, over 60 percent expressed support for both wars. But within two years a shift occurred, in that more people thought the wars a mistake than believed them worthwhile. In the Korean War, disillusionment set in sooner than it did in the Vietnam War, but that is probably because in the Korean conflict there was no preliminary stage; that is, a period in which the United States sent technical assistants or advisers and then at a later stage committed combat troops.

How seriously the American public took the Korean conflict is demonstrated by their responses to the items in Table VI-44, which were asked in the summer of 1950 shortly after the fighting had started. Five years after the end of World War II, twice as many respondents believed that the Korean War marked the beginning of another major international conflict, and over two-thirds said they thought the United States ought to stop Russia, even if it meant setting off a third world war.

VI-7. Percent Saying United States Entry in Korean and Vietnam Wars a Mistake, 1950–1971 (AIPO)

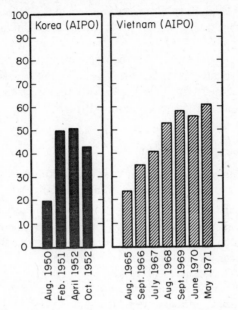

Table VI-44. Korean War, 1950 (AIPO)

Item	Response	
1. Do you think the United States is now actually in World War III, or do you think the present fighting in Korea will stop short of another world war?	In World War III	57%
	Stop short of world war	28
	No opinion	15
2. Which of these two things do you think is more important: that this country keep out of a major war, or that Russian expansion in Asia and Europe be stopped?	Keep out of war	25%
	Stop Russian expansion	68
	No opinion	7

In the fall of 1950, before disillusionment with the war had set in, over 64 percent said they favored continuing the fighting after the North Koreans had been pushed back over the line (38th Parallel) and until they surrendered. When asked whether the United Nations forces should cross the border and fight in China if Chinese troops continued to fight in Korea, almost as many favored as opposed such action: Korea only, 46%; Cross into China, 39%; Don't know, 15%.

But a few months later, the tide had shifted and the American public advocated troop withdrawal and avoidance of conflict with China. The items in Table VI-45 and the distribution of responses describe those shifts in opinion. All of the items in Table VI-45

Table VI-45.   Korean War after Communist China Entered, 1951 (AIPO)

Item	*Response*	
1. Now that Communist China has entered the fighting in Korea with forces far outnumbering the United Nations there, which one of these two courses would you yourself prefer that we follow?	Pull our troops out	66%
	Keep our troops there	25
	No opinion	9
2. Do you think the United States should start an all-out war with Communist China or not?	Should	14%
	Should not	77
	No opinion	9
3. Do you yourself think the United States should or should not try harder to reach an agreement with Communist China or Korea?	Should	56%
	Should not	34
	No opinion	10
4. United Nation forces are trying to push their way back toward the 38th Parallel in Korea. If they succeed in reaching that dividing line (between North and South Korea), do you think we should or should not stop fighting if the Chinese Communists and North Koreans also agree to stop fighting?	Should	73%
	Should not	16
	No opinion	11

appeared in national surveys during the spring of 1951 when, as the data in Graph VI-7 show, at least 50 percent of the public thought our involvement in the Korean conflict a mistake. Responses to these items indicate that the public wished to avoid an encounter with China and was anxious for a negotiated settlement that stopped short of a military victory.

So much for the Korean conflict, which ended finally with a negotiated settlement that left the country divided as it was before, at the 38th Parallel. We turn now to a few comments about attitudes toward the Vietnam War and trace public opinion on questions concerning the extent of American involvement, whether to continue or cease the bombing of North Vietnam, and the conditions for an acceptable peace settlement. By the summer of 1965, it was clear that American troops were assuming a major burden of the fighting. We noted in Graph VI-7 that during that summer, 61 percent believed we had not made a mistake in going into the war, compared to 24 percent who thought we had. But even though more than twice as many supported as opposed the war, most people were pessimistic about its development. In August 1965, 70 percent thought the situation in Vietnam was getting worse, compared to 6 percent who thought it was getting better, 15 percent said the situation was unchanged, and 9 percent had no opinion (AIPO).

In 1965 and 1966, most people responded positively to the idea of submitting the Vietnam question to the United Nations, as shown in Table VI-46. In August 1965, the question read:

> Do you approve or disapprove of the move to ask the United Nations to try to work out its own formula for peace in Vietnam (AIPO)?

In February and September 1966, the question read:

> It has been suggested that the United States agree to submit the case of what to do about Vietnam to the United Nations or to the World Court and agree to accept the decision whatever it happens to be. Do you think this is a good idea or a poor idea (AIPO)?

The decline in support for the idea may have been a consequence of the wording of the question and not a decline in the willingness of the public to have the United Nations try to work out a solution. We

Table VI-46.   Submission of Vietnam Issue to United Nations, 1965-1966 (AIPO)

Month and Year	Approve / Good Idea	Disapprove / Poor Idea	No Opinion
August 1965	74%	13%	13%
February 1966	49	36	15
September 1966	51	32	17

could find no other national polls in which the item appeared after the fall of 1966.

Concerning the bombings of North Vietnam, until President Johnson announced his decision to stop them in March 1968, the public supported the bombings. With slight variations, a typical item about the bombings read as follows:

> In your opinion, should the United States continue the bombing of North Vietnam, or should we stop the bombing (AIPO)?

Table VI-47.   Continuation of United States Bombing of North Vietnam, 1966-1968 (AIPO)

Month and Year	Favor	Oppose	No Opinion
March 1966	61%	26%	13%
February 1967	67	24	9
October 1967	63	26	11
February 1968	70	16	14

The distribution of responses is shown in Table VI-47. Even though 70 percent answered that they approved of the bombings, when asked two months later in April 1968 whether they approved of President Johnson's decision to stop the bombings of North Vietnam, 64 percent said they approved of the President's decision, 26 percent disapproved, and 10 percent had no opinion. These responses probably tell us more about the extent to which the American public supported the administration's policies than about the public's support for specific actions taken by the government to carry out those policies.[10] As suggested in the introductory

[10] This is one of the points that Verba (1970) makes.

remarks to this chapter, providing such a "show of faith" is generally all that the public wishes to do in many areas of foreign policy.

Although it was President Nixon who popularized the phrase "Vietnamization of the war," by which he meant that more of the fighting and over-all burden of the war would be taken over by the South Vietnamese and that American troops would be gradually withdrawn, the public had already indicated it supported such a policy in 1966 and 1967. When the public was asked whether it thought the United States should begin to let South Vietnam take on more responsibility for the fighting in Vietnam, a large majority answered "yes" (AIPO), as shown in Table VI–48.

Table VI–48.   Vietnamization, 1966–1967 (AIPO)

Month and Year	Favor	Oppose	No Opinion
September 1966	62%	22%	16%
September 1967	77	11	12

Even earlier than 1967, the American people had become skeptical about the United States' relationship with the government of South Vietnam. Responses to the items in Table VI–49 are consistent in expressing doubt about the wisdom of the United States tying itself too closely to South Vietnam. In the first three items, the reference is more specifically to the government of South Vietnam; the last item refers to the people of the country. The more even split in public sentiment on the last item as opposed to the others probably reflected greater responsibility for, or sympathy with, the people and a recognition of how weary of the war they must be.

Finally, we comment on two aspects of public opinion about Vietnam: (1) the alternatives that the public supported or would be willing to settle for in order to get American troops out of Vietnam; (2) the public's assessment of President Nixon's handling of the war. On the first point, the most extreme position was one that called for a military victory, even if it became necessary to use atomic weapons. The more moderate position was one that denied the necessity for a military victory. It recommended a compromise, with the country divided into a North and a South Vietnam and

Table VI-49.   Expectations of South Vietnam, 1965-1968 (AIPO)

Item		Response	

1. Do you think the South Vietnamese will be able to establish a stable government or not?		*January 1965*	*May 1966*
	Yes	25%	29%
	No	42	42
	No opinion	33	29

2. If the United States and North Vietnam come to peace terms and United States troops are withdrawn from Vietnam, do you think that a strong enough government can be developed in South Vietnam to withstand Communist pressures?		*June 1967*
	Yes	25%
	No	50
	No opinion	25

3. Suppose the South Vietnamese start fighting on a big scale among themselves. Do you think we should continue to help them, or should we withdraw our troops?		*May 1966*
	Continue to help	28%
	Withdraw our troops	54
	Don't know	18

4. Do you think most of the South Vietnamese want the United States to get out of their country or not?		*March 1968*
	Yes	40%
	No	45
	No opinion	15

each agreeing to recognize the territorial and political integrity of the other. In the items and responses shown in Table VI-50, we note the relative support for each of these positions. It is unfortunate that the first item, which asked for expressions of approval about a military victory, was combined with the issue of whether or not to use atomic weapons. Perhaps, however, that is a realistic way of viewing the problem. As the responses indicate, about 65 percent said they disagreed with the proposal that in order to win an all-out military victory, the United States should use atomic weapons. We note that as early as June 1966, only a small proportion of the public

**Table VI-50. Course of Action to End Vietnam War,
1967–1969 (AIPO)**

Item		Response			
1. Some people say we should go all out to win a military victory in Vietnam, using atom bombs and other atomic weapons. Do you agree or disagree with this view?		*May 1967*		*March 1968*	
	Agree	26%		27%	
	Disagree	64		65	
	No opinion	10		8	

Item		*June 1966*	*October 1967*	*February 1968*	*May 1968*
2. How do you think the war in Vietnam will end—in an all-out victory for the United States and the South Vietnamese, in a compromise peace settlement, or in a defeat for the United States and the South Vietnamese?	Victory	17%	19%	20%	10%
	Compromise	54	64	61	77
	Defeat	6	4	4	4
	No opinion	23	13	15	9

Item		*June 1969*
3. It has been suggested that the United States call for a cease-fire in Vietnam with both sides staying where they now are. Would you approve or disapprove if the United States took this step?	Approve	53%
	Disapprove	34
	No opinion	13

expected that the United States would win an all-out victory and that a majority of the respondents thought that the fighting would stop as a result of a compromise peace settlement. Since 1966, that expectation has increased from 54 to 77 percent.

Only a small proportion of the public was willing to acknowledge that the United States might be defeated in Vietnam. Since

May 1968, there has been more discussion in the mass media about this possibility and commentators have wondered whether or how the United States could face losing its first war. Note that the question asked in June 1969, was not what the American public thought *would* happen, but whether they *approved* or *disapproved* of having the United States call for a cease-fire. The responses showed that this was a favored alternative.

In 1969 and 1970, the problem typically posed was in one of three forms:

> Some United States Senators are saying that we should withdraw all our troops from Vietnam immediately. Do you agree or disagree (AIPO)?
>
> A proposal has been made in Congress to bring home all United States troops from Vietnam before the end of *the year*. Would you like to have your Congressman vote for or against the proposal (AIPO)?
>
> Do you think the United States should or should not withdraw all troops from Vietnam by the end of *next* year (AIPO)?

The results are shown in Table VI-51. Along with the willingness to accept a compromise settlement of the war, the opinion held by a two-thirds majority was that all American troops should be withdrawn from Vietnam by the end of 1971.[11]

Table VI-51. **Withdrawal of United States Troops from Vietnam, 1969-1971 (AIPO)**

Month and Year	Immediate	By End of This Year	By End of Next Year
November 1969	21%	—	—
February 1970	35	—	—
September 1970	—	55	—
November 1970	—	—	61
February 1971	—	66	—

[11]When a similar item was offered on two national surveys in 1970, but one also contained a list of alternative strategies, only 13 and 7 percent favored sending more troops to Vietnam and stepping up the fighting.

On the second point, concerning the extent to which the public endorsed President Nixon's policy, we report two sets of results. The first asked directly:

Do you approve or disapprove of the way President Nixon is handling the situation in Vietnam (AIPO)?

Graph VI-8 shows that from a low of 44 percent in March 1969, support for the President's policies increased until it reached a high of 65 percent in January 1970. Since then, and during the Vietnamese invasion of Cambodia in the spring of 1970, support declined; although as of August 1970 it was at approximately the same level it had been a year earlier.

But looking at this set of figures hides what are stronger criticisms of the Nixon position on Vietnam. For example, when the

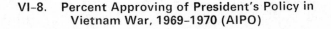

VI-8. Percent Approving of President's Policy in Vietnam War, 1969-1970 (AIPO)

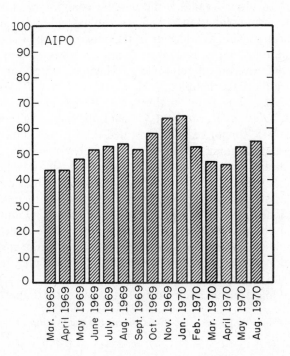

public was asked in February and again in May 1971 whether it thought the Nixon administration was or was not telling the public all it should know about the Vietnam War, 69 and 67 percent said the administration was not (AIPO).[12] And at about the same time, when asked the following question 72 percent said they disagreed with the President.

> Do you agree or disagree with President Nixon that if we leave South Vietnam in a position to defend herself, we will have peace in the next generation (AIPO)?

At the time of writing, the Vietnam War is still going on. It has been extended into Cambodia and Laos. The Nixon administration has been consistent in reiterating that it will be a long war, but one that will result in an honorable settlement. How the public will eventually perceive and evaluate this dismal period in American history remains to be seen and studied at a later time.

The one major theme that comes through most clearly in this review of three decades is the public's commitment to American involvement in international affairs. Having had "star billing" since at least the end of World War II, the public may show some signs—but we think not consistent or significant signs—that it wishes to have its government return to playing "bit parts" or indeed to leaving the stage completely. However optimistic or pessimistic it may feel at any point in time about American-Soviet or Sino-American relations or about Vietnam, the public has consistently, since 1945, supported and advocated that its government play an activist and leading role in world affairs. Even with the misgivings and disappointments that have been voiced by members of the Congress and the public about Vietnam and our China policy, there are no significant signs that the public wishes to return to the isolationist position it held before World War II. On major issues such as the Marshall Plan, atomic weapons, and the United Nations, the public has been more informed and more opinionated than the traditional model of public awareness of foreign policy would have led us to expect.

While foreign affairs may not assume the importance that

[12]These responses were made before the publication of the Pentagon papers.

certain bread-and-butter issues do on the domestic scene, such as farm policy, taxes, or welfare programs, characterizations of the public's relative indifference may no longer accurately describe public sentiment in the present and forthcoming decades.

SUGGESTED READINGS

Acheson, Dean. *Present at the Creation.* New York, 1970

Almond, Gabriel. *The American People and Foreign Policy.* New York, 1950.

Cohen, Bernard. *The Press and Foreign Policy.* Princeton, 1963.

Dickinson, John. "Democratic Realities and Democratic Dogma." *American Political Science Review,* 24 (1930), 283–309.

Inkeles, Alex. *Public Opinion in Soviet Russia.* Cambridge, 1950.

Kelman, Herbert C., ed. *International Behavior.* New York, 1965.

Markel, Lester, ed. *Public Opinion and Foreign Policy.* New York, 1949.

Perkins, Dexter. *America and Two Wars.* Boston, 1944.

Perkins, Dexter. *The American Approach to Foreign Policy.* Cambridge, 1952.

Pool, Ithiel de Sola. *Communications and Values in Relation to War and Peace: Report to the Committee on Research for Peace.* New York, 1961.

Rosenau, James N. *Public Opinion and Foreign Policy: An Operational Formulation.* New York, 1961.

Rovere, Richard, and Arthur Schlesinger, Jr. *The MacArthur Controversy and American Foreign Policy.* New York, 1965.

Smith, Bruce L., and Chitra M. Smith. *International Communication and Public Opinion: A Guide to the Literature.* Princeton, 1956.

Truman, David B. *The Government Process.* New York, 1951.

Verba, Sydney. "The Silent Majority: Myth and Reality." *University of Chicago Magazine*, 63, No. 2 (1970), 10–19.

Verba, Sydney, and Lucien Pye, eds. *Political Culture and Political Development.* Princeton, 1965.

VII
SUMMARY AND
IMPLICATIONS

The purpose of this chapter is to pull together public opinion about major trends in foreign and domestic affairs during the relatively short and homogeneous time periods that were described in detail in the previous chapters. This procedure should help explain the significance of opinion on specific topics through time, as well as the implications of opinions in one area for other problems at issue in the society at the same time. The chapter is divided into five parts that have the following temporal boundaries: (1) the period preceding United States' entry into World War II, roughly from 1936 until the end of 1941; (2) the war years, until Japan's defeat in August 1945; (3) the postwar era, which we extend to the end of the Truman administration in 1952; (4) the Eisenhower period, 1952–1960; and (5) the Kennedy–Johnson–Nixon years, 1960–1970.

THE PREWAR YEARS: 1936–1941

The narrative began in the late 1930's. The United States was in the midst of a depression, and there was uncertainty about whether the nation would be able to avoid involvement in another major European conflict, should one develop. The second term of the New Deal, with its massive program for economic reform and social welfare, was beginning to unfold.

The Wagner or Labor-Industrial Relations Act, the Social Security Act, the Fair Labor Standards Act (minimum-wage/maximum-hour laws), and the Child Labor Act were all enacted during this period. John L. Lewis had recently broken away from the craft-oriented American Federation of Labor and organized the Council for Industrial Organization. The CIO was a new and militant labor movement actively engaged in organizing automobile, steel, and other industrial workers in major industries. The poll data described a nation almost wholly concerned with questions of economic policy and social welfare. It is interesting, for example, that there were no polls, and hardly any single items, about Negroes or civil rights. In my search, I uncovered no items about Negroes but assume that there may have been some that compared the relative power or desirability of Negroes with other ethnic and racial groups (Jews, Germans, Japanese). Negroes during this period were indeed the "invisible minority"—not so the Jews. In retrospect, it turns out that the late 1930's, was the time of strongest interest in anti-Semitism and attitudes toward Jews. In large measure, the interest may have stemmed from the "special treatment" that the Jews were receiving in Nazi Germany. Questions about civil liberties, like civil rights, were also conspicuous by their relative absence. The few items that did appear on national polls were directed primarily at the rights to which members of the Communist Party were entitled.

Turning, then, to those issues about which there was a good deal of interest, we look first at the extent to which the public supported the new social-welfare programs, opinions about trade unions and the power to which the American public considered them entitled, and reactions to events in Europe and Asia.

Until the second term of Franklin Roosevelt's administration, the United States, compared to European industrial nations, had little in the way of government-sponsored welfare programs. Social security, old-age pensions, health programs, minimum-wage laws were all programs that had yet to be enacted or had just recently been adopted. January 1936 was the first time a national poll carried questions about federally financed old-age pensions. At that time, 87 percent of the respondents said they supported such legislation. In the two or three years that followed, whenever the public was asked for its opinion of federal programs that would give financial support to the aged or the sick (who were in need), it responded by indicating almost unanimous approval. But an important strain within this general tone of approval was the belief that only persons *in need* should receive support from the government. Thus, while 81 percent in 1938 said that they thought the government should be responsible for providing medical care for people who were unable to pay for it, it was not until 1961 that a majority of the respondents favored a medical-insurance program administered under social security, in which financial need was not a criterion for service. When the issue was first raised in Truman's administration in 1946, only 12 percent said they favored a medical-insurance program under social security.

Along the same lines, we note that in 1937 and 1938 when the public was asked for its opinion of the proposed and then newly enacted minimum-wage law, over 60 percent said they favored such legislation. In the dozen or so times from 1938 to 1968 that the public was polled on this issue of government-established minimum-wage levels, the proportion who approved of the practice and of the wages established was almost twice as high as those who opposed. Yet, in 1965, when asked to react to a proposal whereby the government would guarantee to provide a family with a minimum annual income, only 19 percent favored the idea, two-thirds were opposed, and the remaining 14 percent had no opinion.

In the 1930's, the public wanted the federal government to concern itself with social welfare on a larger scale than it had in the past. But the public shared the ideology that was implicit in each piece of legislation, which was that social welfare and government services in the fields of health, welfare, and education were not the rightful due of every citizen. They were to be available only to those who could show they were unable to provide for those needs out of their own resources.

Public support for the right of laborers to organize into trade unions was not noticeably greater during this period than it was in later years, when the society was more affluent. The percentage, for example, who said they favored labor unions ranged from 72 in 1936 to 61 in 1941. Over the next two and a half decades, during which this item appeared on at least ten national polls, the proportion of respondents who answered in the affirmative never dropped below 61 percent.

On specific issues and practices of labor unions, the American public was less supportive. In 1937 and 1939, more than twice as many opposed as supported a closed shop. Over 70 percent also opposed a union shop. When A. J. Muste and other militant labor leaders adopted the technique of the sit-down strike—which had been used by the textile workers in Britain in an earlier era— against rubber plants in Akron, Ohio, and the Auto-lite plant in Toledo, the American public voiced strong opposition. In tracing the public's attitudes toward the trade-union movement over the entire time span of the study, we note that opinion remained stable in the degree to which the public supported the right to organize and in its unwillingness to extend support to other activities that organized labor designated as legitimate and essential.

A dramatic reminder of how pervasive the depression was and how deeply it affected decisions on day-to-day activities is reflected in the public's responses to items about the desirability of having children and about ideal family size. When asked early in 1941 what the main reasons were that couples did not have more children, 62 percent said "the cost of living," "we do not have enough money," and "economic uncertainty about the future." Among 86 percent of the respondents the ideal family size in 1936 and 1941 was no more than two children. And within that group, 32 percent answered "no children." Over 75 percent also favored having government health clinics furnish birth-control information to those married people who wanted it.

In his chapter on "Population Growth in the United States," Bogue (1961, p. 137) comments that "when the 1940 census was taken it was discovered that the United States had grown more slowly than at any time in its history—7.2 per cent." Later (p. 681), Bogue states: "During the years of the economic depression, the total fertility rate was only slightly above 2 children per completed family."

The tense situation in Europe, as Hitler consolidated his power in Germany and then sought to extend it to neighboring countries, added to the mood of uncertainty and fear that characterized public opinion in the 1930's. The main thrust of the questions about foreign affairs during this period focused on the wisdom of American involvement in "European conflicts." Had American involvement been a mistake in 1917, and would it be a mistake to consider involvement again? In 1937, 66 percent said they thought it had been a mistake for the United States to enter World War I; 95 percent said that if another war like World War I were to develop in Europe, the United States should not take part; and only 26 percent supported the idea of the United States joining a world organization "with police power to maintain world peace."[1]

Between 1937 and December 1941, the American public had a change of heart about the wisdom of United States participation in World War I, and the percentage who believed it a mistake declined from 64 to 39. But on the matter of whether the United States ought to get involved a second time, there was no significant shift of opinion. Two months before Pearl Harbor, 79 percent said that if given the opportunity to vote about whether to go into or stay out of the war, they would vote to stay out.[2] Franklin Roosevelt's Presidential campaign of 1940 was reminiscent of Woodrow Wilson's campaign of 1916. In essence, both promised that American boys would not be sent overseas to fight in "Europe's wars."

In 1939, 69 percent of the American public opposed lending money to England and France so that they could buy airplanes and other war materials. But as attitudes toward Germany grew increasingly negative between 1939 and the end of 1941, so did feelings of friendship and dependency develop toward Britain.[3] In 1937, two-thirds of those polled had characterized the German people as "essentially peace-loving and kindly, who have been unfortunate in being misled by ruthless and ambitious rulers." In March 1940, 75 percent said they thought England and France should meet with Germany and try to end the war. In November 1940, 54 percent believed that we should find some way of "continuing our European commercial business with Hitler's new Europe." But by April 1941, only 16 percent said they favored a peace between Britain and Germany which assumed that Germany

[1] In April 1938, when asked if they thought the United States would have to fight Germany in their lifetime 54 percent answered "no."

[2] As indicated in Chapter VI, this figure does not mean that the public did not understand that the chances of the United States being able to stay out were growing more and more dim as events in Europe changed. Indeed, by November 1941, only 15 percent said they thought the United States would be *able* to stay out of another world war.

[3] Nevertheless, when the lend-lease arrangements with Britain were introduced on the floor of the Congress, they faced strong opposition and were debated for many weeks.

could keep some of the territory it had acquired by conquest.

The public's increasing hostility toward Germany for plunging Europe, and almost inevitably the United States, into another and even more bitter international conflict than that which had occurred two decades earlier could reasonably have been expected to have some effect on public opinion concerning Germany's treatment of its Jewish community. The repercussions might even have been expected to extend to feelings about American Jews.

Although 94 percent said they disapproved of the Nazis' treatment of the Jews, when asked whether Jews were partly or entirely responsible for their own persecution and for the hostility that non-Jews felt toward them, the percentages that were negative toward the Jews were two and three times as great as the percentages that indicated positive or favorable attitudes. Moreover, 71 percent opposed the entry in large numbers of Jewish exiles from Germany. Compared to Englishmen, Swedes, Russians, Chinese, and Mexicans, Jews were perceived as less desirable immigrants.

On the whole, American disapproval of the Nazis' treatment of German Jewry had little carryover to attitudes about Jews in the United States. Disapproval of the policy of the Nazi regime did not alter negative perceptions of Jews who were the victims of that policy, nor did such policy make Jews appear less blameworthy in the eyes of the American public. During the depression—perhaps in part *because* of the depression and the image that the American public held of the financial ability of Jews, coupled with a belief that they were more aggressive and unscrupulous in business affairs than non-Jews—anti-Semitism was a more widespread phenomenon than in any subsequent period in American history including the present time.

By the fall of 1940, attitudes toward Germany had become increasingly negative, but the public's mood concerning Japan changed more slowly. Between November 1940 and December 1941, when asked whether it was time for the United States to take strong measures against Japan, those who said "yes" amounted to 49 percent in November 1940, 51 percent in July 1941, and 60 percent in December 1941, only days before the attack on Pearl Harbor.[4] In October 1941, more Americans advocated a wait-and-

[4]The item at that time read: "Should the United States take steps now to keep Japan from becoming more powerful, even if this means risking a war with Japan?"

see policy toward Japan than supported a confrontation or a more provocative stance in the Pacific. By the summer of 1939, sympathy was clearly with China as opposed to Japan (74 percent said they were more sympathetic to China, 2 percent said to Japan, and the remaining 24 percent said "neither side"), but the United States was neither psychologically nor militarily prepared to contemplate a war with Japan. Even as late as the fall of 1941, majority sentiment advocated the adoption of a strong "political" line vis-à-vis Japan and punitive economic policies involving boycotts of Japanese goods and embargoes on the shipment of scrap iron and war materials. But the American public was not urging its government to provoke an incident that would lead to war.

Prepared or not, willing or apathetic, Americans were at war two months later. The next section summarizes public opinion during the period of American involvement in World War II.

THE WAR YEARS: 1941–1945

From the outset, almost everyone expected the Allies to win.[5] But they thought it would be a long war—longer than World War I. In January 1942, no one thought it would last less than a year; 38 percent thought it would last three years or longer; 29 percent, more than two years; and 21 percent, between one and two years (12 percent had no opinion). Six months later, the percentage who thought the war would last between one and two years increased to 35 percent, and the percentage who thought three or more years dropped to 29. In the beginning, Germany was perceived as the major enemy, but by September 1943, the ranking was reversed and twice as many said they thought Japan posed the major threat.

Among the nations that were allies of the United States during the war, none received more attention from the polls than the Soviet Union. Before the war, most Americans had been skeptical of the degree of cooperation that could be worked out between their government and Russia; but after the United States was directly involved in the war, the public seemed more willing to put aside ideological disagreements and to treat the Russians as full partners.

[5]In January 1942, 7 percent said they thought the Axis powers would win, and 16 percent did not know.

For example, when asked in October 1941 and then again in February 1942 what policy the United States ought to pursue vis-à-vis the Soviet Union, the percentage who advocated treating Russia as a full partner increased from 22 to 41 percent.

In June 1943, 81 percent said they thought we should try to work with Russia as an equal partner in fighting the war. The crucial phrase in that item is "in fighting the war," because while 81 percent answered that they were willing to treat Russia as an equal partner in that context, most of them also said that they anticipated trouble with the Soviet Union after the war. For example, 48 as compared to 31 percent thought Russia would make demands at the peace table that we could not agree to. And when asked whether the United States should make a permanent military alliance with Britain, the Soviet Union, and/or China, 61 percent said "yes with Britain," 56 percent said "yes with China," and 39 percent said "yes with the Soviet Union." On the other hand, more than twice as many (48 compared to 22 percent) thought we would get along better with the Soviet Union after the war than before the war.

Unfortunately, there were no national polls during the war concerning American attitudes toward the Communist Party in the United States. From other sources, however, such as newspapers and movies, the number of organizations collecting money for Russian war relief, and the enormous increase in membership of such groups as the American-Soviet Friendship Council, the Joint Anti-Fascist League, and the American Youth for Democracy, we know of the success of the popular front in the United States. These data are in contrast to what public attitudes toward the Communist Party had been as late as October 1941. For example, the public was asked at that time, "What, if anything, do you believe should be done about communists in the United States?" Of the 89 percent with an opinion, only 5 percent said "do nothing"; 54 percent wanted to regulate communists' behavior by having them register with the government or to deny them "a say in the government" or "some sort of control," and 30 percent favored more drastic action, such as deportation or internment in camps. In June 1941, 71 percent said they favored making membership in the Communist Party illegal.[6] The American public adopted much the same stand

[6]At the time the June poll was taken, the Stalin-Hitler pact was still operative and thus the Soviet Union was an "inactive" supporter of Nazi Germany.

vis-à-vis its domestic communists within a year after the end of the war.

The idea that the war should be fought until Germany and Japan surrendered unconditionally met with widespread approval. On the three or four occasions that the public had a chance to express its opinion on the strategy of surrender, over 75 percent urged that fighting continue until Germany was "crushed" or until Germany and Japan surrendered "unconditionally." Concerning the extent to which German citizens were held responsible for the treatment that civilian prisoners received, over 80 percent said they thought that the German people approved entirely or partly of the killing and starving of prisoners in Germany. Also, 48 percent said they thought many among the German civilian population knew about the atrocities in prison camps while the war was still going on.

When the American public was asked in December 1944 and then again in May 1945 whether it believed the stories about the number of people who had been murdered in the concentration camps, 76 and 84 percent answered "yes"; but of those who said they thought the stories were true, the figure most often cited was 100,000 or less. In May 1945, the number cited by half of the respondents was 1,000,000. According to the figures reported by the Allied governments and by Jewish sources, if the estimate of 1,000,000 was multiplied ninefold, it would come close to the actual number killed.

The underestimating of the number of people killed in German concentration camps is probably related to the attitudes expressed by the public concerning Hitler's treatment of the Jews. When asked in 1942, 1943, and 1944 whether Hitler did the right thing in taking away the power of the Jews in Germany and why he did so, a majority of the respondents (62 and 58 percent) believed it was wrong, but a sizable minority either were ambivalent about the deed or had no opinion. Furthermore, 49 percent gave reasons that were categorized by the pollsters as anti-Semitic, in response to the question "Why do you think Hitler took away the power of the Jews in Germany?" And in 1943, 29 percent said they thought the news that 2,000,000 Jews had been killed in Europe since the war began was a rumor, 24 percent had no opinion on the question, and 47 percent thought it was true.

In Chapter IV we reported that in 1961, 59 percent of the

American public said that the Eichmann trial (with its rehashing of Nazi policy toward the Jews, conditions in the camps, atrocities committed, and so on) had no effect on their feelings toward the Jewish people. The data described above and in the previous section on responses toward the Nazis' treatment of the Jews in the late 1930's confirm the public's assessment of its own feelings. There was a sharp reduction in anti-Semitism in the United States in the decades of the 1950's and 1960's, but it is evident that the reduction did not come about as a direct result of the victimization of the Jews by the Nazis. Further evidence for this conclusion is shown in the public's responses to Truman's proposals in the fall of 1945 to loosen immigration policies for Jewish and other victims of the Nazi regime. In whatever form the proposals were presented (the United States ought to share with other nations the responsibility for absorbing a given number of refugees, change the immigration quotas, or accept many displaced persons), most people opposed them. In 1945, 72 percent said they disapproved of a change in the immigration laws so that more Jewish and other refugees could come to the United States to live.

In the 1930's, when this idea was first suggested, one could argue that given the depressed state of the American economy even though the public might have felt a good deal of compassion for the victims, the reality of millions already unemployed at home was too strong a deterrent. But this was clearly not the situation in 1945. The fear that there would be a depression in the next few years is also not a powerful explanation. Thus we conclude that during the war the American public favored harsh treatment toward its enemies, in large measure held the citizenry of the two major powers involved responsible for their governments' behavior, and supported the verdicts handed down at Nuremberg against the leaders of the Nazi regime. But these opinions had little carryover to the victims of those policies.

Feeling ran deep against the Japanese living in the United States.[7] When West Coast residents were asked (one year after Pearl Harbor) whether they would be willing to hire Japanese servants to work in their homes after the war, 49 percent said "no"; and in January 1945, 61 percent said that they did not think Japa-

[7]Unfortunately, we could find no comparable items about attitudes toward Germans in the United States during the war.

nese living in the United States should have as good a chance as white people to get any kind of job.

Another important indicator of the strength of anti-Japanese feeling may be observed by the attitudes expressed toward the dropping of the atomic bombs. Within days after the bombs had been used, the public was asked whether it approved or disapproved of their use; 85 percent approved. It is startling that only 5 percent had no opinion on an event as awesome and complex as the production and use of atomic weapons.

Toward the end of the war, over two-thirds of the American public favored strict supervision of the defeated powers. One-third advocated destroying Germany as a political entity, and 14 percent thought all the Japanese should be killed.

By 1945, the American public was acting as if it had learned a lesson from its government's behavior following World War I; namely, that it was neither possible nor desirable for the United States to adopt an isolationist stance toward the rest of the world. Winning the war in 1918 gained the nation little in the way of international influence or lasting security in the postwar era. This time the public was prepared to behave differently. We noted in Chapter VI that when asked whether the United States ought to join a world organization, the percentage who answered "yes" increased from 26 percent in 1937 to 81 percent in 1945. During the war, over 70 percent consistently answered that they thought it would be best for the future of the United States if the government were to take an active part in world affairs. Thus the prevailing mood in the United States toward the end of the war was that of a nation determined to defeat its enemies and to assure itself a lasting and secure peace.

On the domestic scene, it was during the war that the question of the integration of Negroes into American society was discussed more openly and with greater expressions of concern on the part of more white people than had been heard since the era following the Civil War. The Negro began to lose his invisibility vis-à-vis white society during the years that the United States was fighting nations that had highly developed racist ideologies. Cynical as it sounds, there is probably a good deal of truth in the observation that Americans found themselves caught up in their own propaganda against racism. The policy of segregation in the armed forces, as well as in the schools, in public transportation, and in other spheres became sources of embarrassment to the United States in light of the rhetoric it had adopted against the racist philosophies of its enemies. Thus, for the first time, questions were posed in national polls concerning the rights and opportunities of Negroes in the United States and the legitimacy of the policy of segregation.

In June 1942, the following item appeared for the first time on a national poll:

> In general, do you think Negroes are as intelligent as white people; that is, can they learn just as well if they are given the same education (and training) (NORC)?

At that time, 42 percent said "yes," 48 percent said "no," and 10 percent had no opinion. As we indicated in Chapter III, responses to this item about Negroes, more than any other, showed the greatest shift in public opinion. In two decades, the percentage who answered "yes" had increased by almost 100 percent. On the matter of segregation in schools, public transportation, and neighborhoods, in 1942, 30 percent said that they approved of whites and Negroes going to the same schools, 44 percent favored the integration of streetcars and buses, and 35 percent said it would make no difference to them if a Negro with just as much income and education were to move into their block. In 1944, the public was asked whether Negroes should have as good a chance as white people to get any kind of job or whether white people should have the first chance; 42 percent said they thought Negroes should have as good a chance as white people. Between the early 1940's, when these items appeared on national polls for the first time, and the next two or three decades, the shifts in opinions were always toward more integration and more equality of opportunity, and the amount of change was always great—greater than on any of the other items about Negroes and their civil rights.

One of the requests that the Roosevelt administration had made of trade unions during the war was that they refrain from striking any of the major industries: auto, steel, coal, railroads, and the like. All of the major union leaders gave the President the pledge he requested, with the exception of John L. Lewis and the United Mine Workers. Lewis refused to go along with his colleagues in the labor movement and led the United Mine Workers out of the CIO into a separate and independent union organization. There were no items on national surveys that sought public attitudes toward Roosevelt's request or Lewis's answer; but in February 1944 the public was asked whether it thought a law ought to be passed that would make it unlawful to strike under any circumstances in peacetime, and 24 percent answered "yes" to that proposal (12 percent said they did not know, and 64 percent were opposed). It is reasonable to conclude that if 24 percent favored forbidding strikes during peacetime that a higher proportion would have supported the voluntary strike ban during the war. We know also that within three years after the end of the war, a major piece of labor legislation, the Taft-Hartley Act, was enacted over the organized and strong opposition of the trade unions. The major purpose of the Taft-Hartley Act was to limit the power of organized labor. The data reported in Chapter II demonstrate that the law received widespread public support.

On the other domestic issues, public opinion remained relatively conservative, compared to other Western democracies, such as Britain or the Scandinavian countries, on the matter of government-sponsored welfare programs. When asked whether they favored a cradle-to-grave program of minimum security for all people in the United States, 59 percent said they thought such a program undesirable (three-quarters of whom also thought it economically impossible). Of the 41 percent who thought it desirable, only 20 percent also thought it economically possible. When the issue of a national health program was presented to the American public by the Truman administration right after the war, most people opposed it and advocated doing nothing, working through voluntary insurance plans such as Blue Cross, or leaving the problem to private and community charities.

The mood of the country at the end of the war favored moving slowly in the area of social-economic reform, exercising control on some of the institutions and groups that may have benefited economically from the war, and not embarking on major changes in the institutional structure of American life. The public sensed that the postwar era would pose problems and challenges on issues about which the government had had little prior experience, and the resolutions of which would be important to success in its new role as a major world power.

THE POSTWAR YEARS OF THE TRUMAN ADMINISTRATION: 1945-1952

Among the major domestic challenges facing the United States following the end of the war was the maintenance of its economy at a level of full employment and the expansion of its welfare services within the ideological context of a traditionally capitalist society. Civil rights for Negroes and other minority groups was a more salient issue in postwar America than it had been at any other time in the twentieth century. On the foreign scene, the United States had to come to grips with the relatively new and complicated issue of massive foreign aid (to which countries and under what circumstances), to its role in the United Nations, and to the kind of relationship it would maintain with its wartime ally, the Soviet Union, which had also emerged at the end of the war a much more influential and powerful nation than it had been in 1940. Perhaps most complicated of all was the fact that just prior to the end of the war the United States demonstrated that it had learned how to harness nuclear energy, and in 1945 it was the only country in the world to have produced and used an atomic bomb.

The American public did not seem prepared to make penetrating or important changes in the structure of its society. It seemed anxious to preserve that which had been working well during the war years and to maintain the sense of economic well-being that had been developed during the war. In 1947, a major piece of legislation was enacted that limited the power of labor unions. When the public was asked for its opinion about many of the major provisions in the Taft-Hartley Act—jurisdictional strikes, cooling-off periods, closed shops, featherbedding, secret ballots—it expressed strong support for regulations that opposed the interests of the trade unions. Even on an issue as fundamental as the right of organized labor to bargain collectively, the public was not strongly supportive: 45 percent said they thought that an employer should be required by law to bargain collectively with whatever union was elected by the majority of his workers, but 31 percent thought he should not be, and 24 percent had no opinion.

In the same vein, on as seemingly noncontroversial an issue as whether social security should be extended so that more people could receive payments, 48 percent favored extension, but 32 percent wished to leave the law as it was, and 14 percent had no opinion. These were responses to an issue about which only four years earlier 94 percent had indicated general approval. When the public was given the opportunity to choose between the health-insurance program offered by the Truman administration and the plan proposed by the American Medical Association, 47 percent favored the AMA plan, compared to 33 percent for the government's program. The public believed that the quality of medical care would not be as high under the government's plan.

Unlike social security and federally sponsored health programs, the issue of federal aid to education had received relatively little attention before the war. One aspect of the problem was how much of the burden for primary and secondary public-school education ought to be assumed by the federal government and how much by the state governments. After 1954, the issue became more complicated because then a decision had to be reached about whether the federal government ought to continue supporting public schools that were not abiding by the Supreme Court ruling to integrate "with all deliberate speed." It was not until the 1960's that the issue of federal support to parochial schools was fully aired, although there had been some testing of opinion on this matter in 1938 and in 1947.

On the first part, that of federal versus state aid to public schools, between 55 and 65 percent indicated a willingness to have the federal government help finance public education. Support for federal aid to parochial schools was not as widespread. In 1949, respondents were divided almost evenly between those who supported federal aid to parochial schools and those who opposed it. As indicated in the discussion of this issue that appeared in Chapter II, the question was aired most fully during the Kennedy administration. Kennedy, the country's first Catholic President, opposed federal aid to parochial schools, but his views were overruled by the Congress.

In contrast to the war years, once the sense of national emergency was over, the public "reverted to form" in its attitudes toward taxes, which was that the government was demanding too high a portion of its wages and salaries. We noted in 1944 and 1945 that 90 and 85 percent of the respondents said that they thought the federal income tax that they were required to pay was about right.

But between 1946 and 1952, the proportion who answered "about right" ranged from 62 to 26 percent; the others said that taxes were too high. On the other hand, even though between 1947 and 1949, 75 percent said they opposed tax increases, when asked in 1950 whether they agreed that taxes must be increased immediately to pay for the war in Korea, of those with an opinion, the ratio was almost two to one in favor of raising taxes (20 percent said they did not know).

A striking change that occurred in American attitudes in the years following the end of the war in contrast to the prewar depression era was the public's desire to have more children. In 1947 and 1948, between 35 and 47 percent said they thought that four or more children comprised the ideal number per family. In the 1930's and during the war, less than 10 percent wanted four children and over 50 percent thought that one child or none was the ideal family unit. In the late 1940's, concerns about a population explosion had not yet filtered through to either the mass media or the public consciousness. The years of economic and emotional insecurity were past, and the public manifested its faith in the future by supporting the idea of large families.

Civil rights had been a central theme in Truman's 1948 Presidential campaign. Even though most of the Southern Democrats had bolted the Democratic Party and formed their own Dixiecrat Party, because of Truman's insistence on making civil rights an important national issue in the Presidential campaign, there were relatively few important pieces of legislation enacted that affected the rights of Negroes during Truman's administration.[8] There was much discussion about civil rights, and organizations like the National Association for the Advancement of Colored People, the Urban League, and the Congress on Racial Equality made large gains in membership, money, and attention. But it was not until the middle 1950's that first the appellate courts and then the Congress significantly altered the legal and social status of American Negroes. Some small changes in the attitudes of white Americans could be observed during this period, and they were in the direction of greater willingness to recognize Negroes as having the same rights

[8] The two most significant actions were the issuance of two executive orders in the summer of 1948, in which Truman ordered the desegregation of the armed forces and the ending of discrimination in federal employment.

as other Americans. But only 47 percent said that they thought Negroes should have as good a chance as white people to get any kind of job, and only one-third believed that the federal government should go "all the way" in requiring employers to hire people without regard to race and religion. More than 50 percent said the federal government should have nothing to do with the issue or should leave it to the state governments. President Truman was unable to get a Fair Employment Practices Act through the Congress.

On the whole, if one compares the level of public support and the extent to which the Congress cooperated with the President in enacting New Deal versus Fair Deal legislation, the former had more popular support and much greater success in the legislature. It must be remembered that President Roosevelt had the "advantages" of a depressed economy and massive unemployment, whereas President Truman presented his Fair Deal program during a period of affluence. Thus while the 1930's witnessed the enactment of social security, minimum-wage legislation, public-works laws, and protection to organized labor, many of the major proposals of the Fair Deal program, such as national health insurance, federal aid to education, and civil rights were defeated by the Congress and failed to achieve widespread popular support.

For different reasons both civil liberties and attitudes toward Jews became enmeshed in foreign-policy decisions. The civil-liberties issue was related to American policy vis-à-vis the Soviet Union, which in turn affected treatment of the Communist Party in the United States. The late 1940's and early 1950's coincided with the rise and influence of Senator Joseph McCarthy, who established his career in the Senate on the issue of ferreting out communists and communist sympathizers, broadly defined, from the State Department, the Department of Defense, policy-making bodies around the President, universities, and anywhere else he could find them. Many of the questions involving civil liberties during this period were connected with the rights of political groups in the United States that had ties of various magnitudes to the Soviet Union.

The second topic, that of attitudes toward Jews, was related to American policy vis-à-vis refugees in the displaced-persons camps in Europe, the establishment of the state of Israel, and the stand the United States adopted when war broke out between Arabs and Jews in the Middle East.

On the first topic, that of the connection between opinion about the Soviet Union and opinion on civil liberties, we reported that in 1946, 52 percent said they did not expect Russia to cooperate with the United States in world affairs. Moreover, 62 percent said that the best way to deal with Russia was to keep strong ourselves and to make concessions only when we got something in return. From the fall of 1947 to September 1949, the public was asked on four separate occasions whether it thought the United States was being too soft or too tough in its policy toward Russia. Between 73 and 53 percent (the lowest figure was in September 1949) said they thought the United States was being too soft; 10 percent or less thought we were being too tough.

On the domestic scene, when the public was asked to characterize the loyalties of members of the Communist Party, among those with an opinion (between 20 and 30 percent in 1946 and 1948 did not have an opinion), more than twice as many said that should war break out between the United States and the Soviet Union, American Communists were more likely to be loyal to the Soviet Union than to the United States. Given the image that the public had of Communist Party members, perhaps it is not surprising that in 1948, 80 percent said that if the United States found itself at war with the Soviet Union, members of the Communist party should be imprisoned, shot, or deported. Among the specific activities that at least two-thirds of the American public believed Communist Party members should be excluded from were working in a defense plant, teaching in a high school, and clerking in a store.

These data do not permit us to interpret whether the attitudes expressed on these issues were causal factors in how the public responded to the charges, appeals, and rhetoric of Senator McCarthy. But they do indicate that an environment receptive to the Senator's accusations already existed by 1948-1949. Undoubtedly, the Senator himself helped create that environment. But whether he was a more significant factor than were the policies pursued by the Russian or American government after the war or by the Communist Party within the United States, we cannot clearly discern. We did show that by the summer of 1950, among two-thirds of the public polled who had an opinion, twice as many approved as disapproved of Senator McCarthy and the charges he made.

Now we shift from attitudes toward domestic Communists to

the public's appraisal of the Soviet Union and of American policy vis-à-vis the Soviet government. The mood seems to have been that the United States must remain militarily prepared and should adopt a firm policy toward the Soviet government. These attitudes were manifested particularly in discussions about Berlin. When asked in 1948 and 1949 whether the United States should avoid trouble by pulling American troops and officials out of Berlin, over 75 percent wanted the troops to stay. The same level of support for maintaining troops in Berlin was manifested in 1958, 1959, and 1961. In making more explicit what it meant by a policy of firmness, the public emphasized military preparedness, tough rhetoric, and strong alliances. It stopped short of seeking or encouraging war with the Soviet Union.

The second major sphere in which foreign and domestic issues became entwined concerned Jewish refugees, support for the establishment of the state of Israel, and attitudes toward the American Jewish community. While 89 percent of the respondents who had heard of the Nuremberg trials believed that the sentences imposed on Nazi war criminals were either too lenient or about right, and over 80 percent said that they thought the information about how prisoners had been treated in the concentration camps was true, there seemed to be no carryover to attitudes about the acceptance of refugees, that is, the victims of Nazi policy, into the United States. In 1946, 71 percent did not think the United States should take any displaced Polish, Jewish, or other persons who needed to find new homes because of the Nazis. About 65 percent said they favored the United Nations resolution that two independent states, one Arab and one Jewish, be established out of the British Mandate of Palestine; but when asked which side they would sympathize with should war break out between Jews and Arabs in Palestine, 38 percent said they would be neutral in their feelings and 26 percent had no opinion. Of the approximately one-third with an opinion, twice as many said they would sympathize with the Jews. Along the same lines, when asked, six months after the partition plan was aired, whether they approved of it, 43 percent had no opinion and 31 percent favored trying some other solution. Only 26 percent approved of the partition proposal which led to the establishment of an independent Jewish state. Moreover, 90 percent favored an arms embargo against both Jews and Arabs.

We have other evidence, however, which indicates that there was a sharp decline in anti-Semitic sentiments in the United States between 1945 and 1950. We noted, for example, that when asked "Have you heard any criticism or talk against the Jews in the last six months?" in 1944, 60 percent said "yes"; in 1946, 64 percent said "yes"; but in 1950, the figure dropped to 24 percent; and from then until 1959 (the last time the item was asked), the percentage who answered "yes" did not exceed 21. One cannot help but assume that the events in Europe preceding and during World War II must have influenced public opinion about Jews in the direction of reducing anti-Semitic sentiment. The data suggest that the events did affect opinion toward American Jews, but not toward those Jews who were direct victims of the Nazis. The latter, of course, were people with whom the American public had little or no contact.

Other major issues in American foreign policy during this period centered around the development of a position on the testing and control of atomic weapons, the newly established government on the mainland of China, and foreign aid. The Korean War began toward the end of the period under review.

Concerning the dropping of atomic bombs on Japan, 85 percent said they approved. Most respondents thought the act shortened the war by at least six months. In the two years or so immediately following the end of the war, when knowledge and appreciation of the enormity of atomic power must have only slowly seeped through to the consciousness of the American public, majority sentiment favored doing everything possible to maintain a monopoly over knowledge of how to produce the bomb: 71 percent were opposed to sharing the secret, and 66 percent said they did not want observers from other nations on the scene when the United States made tests of atomic weapons.

Initially (July 1946) when the Baruch Plan for international inspection of atomic weapons was first suggested, more respondents opposed than favored the plan. By May 1948, there was a slight shift in sentiment (perhaps because by then the Russians were also producing atomic bombs), such that 43 percent favored inspection and 39 percent opposed; the other 18 percent were undecided. In January 1948, 78 percent said that the United States should agree to stop making atomic bombs before an international agency was set up. But in 1950, when the American public was asked whether the United States should go ahead and try to make a hydrogen bomb which might be up to a thousand times more powerful than the atomic bomb, 69 percent said we should go ahead. Another 9 percent said we should make the bomb but use it only as a last resort—a somewhat tautological position. In the next section, we report what appears to be a shift in American sentiment on producing, testing, and sharing information of atomic weapons.

We noted in Chapter VI that one of the important topics about which there was a significant dearth of information was the attitude of the American people toward China. The picture that emerged from the scanty evidence available showed widespread ignorance or indifference about Chiang Kai-shek's regime and about whether it would be able to withstand a Communist takeover. In 1949, 44 percent said they had no opinion about Chiang Kai-shek or about whether the United States ought to do anything to stop China from going Communist. Those with opinions were more likely to be negative toward Chiang and opposed to the United States doing anything. It is interesting, however, that although there was this widespread ignorance and indifference, more than twice as many opposed rather than favored United States recognition of the Communist regime. When asked in September 1950 whether the Communist government of China should be permitted to have the council seat of the Nationalist government on the United Nations Security Council, 8 percent said "yes," 58 percent said "no," and the remainder had no opinion. A decade or so later, the proportion who opposed increased to 63 percent, and the proportion who favored increased to 20 percent. At no time from 1950 until 1970–1971 was there more than about 30 percent support for any action that would result in bringing the Communist government of China into closer contact with the United States or with the community of nations represented in the United Nations. The "no opinion" and "undecided" respondents of the late 1940's and early 1950's shifted into the anti-China group later in the decade.

Opinions about China were also expressed, although somewhat indirectly, in connection with the Korean conflict. Korea, like Vietnam, was not a popular war. An important factor that contributed to the negative feelings was the presence of Chinese troops in Korea. At the beginning of the conflict, when asked whether the United States had made a mistake in going into the war, 20 percent said "yes." In the next year and a half the percentage of respondents who perceived American involvement in Korea as a mistake more than doubled. The public felt strongly that even though there were both American and Chinese soldiers in Korea, the United States should not get involved in a war with China. In the fall of 1951, 66 percent said we should pull our troops out of Korea as fast as possible now that the Chinese Communists had entered the fighting in Korea in significant numbers. Indeed, 77 percent opposed an all-out war with China, and 73 percent believed that we should stop fighting when the United Nations forces reach the 38th Parallel, assuming that the Chinese Communists and North Koreans would also agree to stop fighting at that position.

A final observation on foreign policy during this period concerns the public's willingness to support foreign-aid programs. The massive economic and military programs involving aid to European, Latin American, and Asian nations that began in the period immediately following the end of World War II were unique in American or, perhaps, in any nation's history. We noted that right after the war (in October 1945), when the public was first asked whether the United States should lend the Soviet Union and Britain five or six billion dollars to help them get back on their feet, 60 percent disapproved and 27 percent approved. Respondents were no more willing to help Britain than they were Russia. But within a couple of years, there was a significant shift in opinion, probably in large measure because of the intensive educational campaign the Truman administration waged concerning the importance to American security of foreign aid. By the summer of 1950, 60 percent supported the Marshall Plan, and in 1949 and 1950, when asked "In general do you think it is a good policy for the United States to try to help backward countries to raise their standard of living?" about 75 percent said "yes." At the same time, 70 percent answered "yes" when asked whether they thought such help to backward countries would help the United States should a war break out.

There have been occasions between 1949 and the present when support for foreign aid waned from the 75 percent reported above. But on the whole, the American public responded as if it recognized that providing massive military and economic aid to friendly and/or less developed nations was one of the responsibilities that a major power must assume.

THE EISENHOWER YEARS: 1952-1960

A supreme Court decision destroying the legitimacy of the segregated school system that had prevailed in the South since the end of Reconstruction, the decline of McCarthyism and the attendant concerns over civil liberties, the end of the Korean War, the crisis over Berlin, and the continued testing of nuclear weapons by the major powers were the themes around which many national polls were organized during the period in which the Republicans held national office for the first time in twenty years.

The Supreme Court's decision on school desegregation opened the way for test cases that led to the eventual demise of the "separate but equal" doctrine and forbade segregation in public transportation, housing, recreational facilities, and almost all aspects of public life. This total rejection of the legitimacy of segregated facilities occurred by the end of the Republican administration, but it took another decade before integration on a broad scale had been achieved in the South and in parts of the North. In discussing the civil-rights movement, many commentators have referred to the "revolutionary role" played by the Supreme Court.[9] It was the Court, they claimed, that led public opinion in the acceptance of the social changes that followed upon its decisions. Unlike previous eras in American history, the Court on this issue did not reflect, slowly or grudgingly, popular sentiment or legislative enactments, but indeed led in the formation of attitudes conducive to the rulings it made.

Between July 1954 (only two months after the Court's decision in *Brown v. Board of Education*) and July 1959, the national polls sought public opinion on the Court's decision at least eight times. During this period, the percentage who answered that they approved of the decision ranged from 54 to 63 percent (the high occurred in January 1957). While these figures represent majority sentiment for the nation as a whole, when the question was phrased "Would you object to having your children attend a school where the *majority* of pupils are Negroes?" the percentage who objected *outside* the South ranged from 45 to 60.[10] In the South, the percentage who

[9]See, for example, Waskow (1966), esp. Chap. XVI, pp. 276-290; and Kalven (1965).

[10]This version was asked only of parents of children attending elementary and high school.

objected ranged from 62 to 86 percent.

We noted in Chapter III that in the ten years between the first time the question about the native intelligence of Negroes was asked (in 1946) and the second time (in 1956), there was an increase of almost 100 percent in the proportion who thought Negroes were as intelligent as whites. While not many Negro children were attending newly integrated public schools two years after the Court's decree, the fact that some were may explain much of that 100 percent increase. The same large shifts in opinion in the direction of favoring desegregation of public transportation facilities and residential areas also occurred between the 1940's and the "post-1954 fifties."

Unlike previous periods, the 1950's was not a time when there was much interest in anti-Semitism in the United States. The absence of inquiry suggests that both the phenomenon and its study belonged to an era that had ended with the passing of the Nazi regime—at least for the American public.[11] As indicated in the previous section of this chapter, the proportion of people who answered that they had heard criticism or talk against the Jews in the preceding six months dropped sharply between 1946 and 1950, and continued to drop throughout the decade of the 1950's. In 1959, only 12 percent said they had heard talk against the Jews.

Stimulated by the impact of Senator Joseph McCarthy, various groups and organizations in the United States became increasingly concerned by the seeming willingness of the American public to permit violations of due process when the targets were persons and institutions whose loyalties to the United States were suspect. The phrases "witch-hunt," "red scare," and "star-chamber proceedings" appeared with regularity in the liberal press and monthly magazines. But the McCarthy "hearings" continued and seemed to attract more and more attention, if not support.

In 1953, the Carnegie Foundation financed a national survey of public attitudes toward political deviance; a summary of some of the pertinent results appeared in Chapter V. At least a few of the findings are worth emphasizing. One is that the public distinguished

[11]When the number of questions included on national polls pertaining to anti-Semitism were compared over different time periods, we noted that there was a decline between the 1936-1945 era, when 35 questions were reported, and the 1956-1965 period, when 20 questions were included.

among different types of political deviancy and rather consistently ranked groups as to which were most and least tolerable. On most matters, socialists (in the tradition of Norman Thomas's American Socialist Party) were best tolerated, and persons whose loyalties were questioned but who denied the charges ranked second. After these two categories there was a sharp decline in the public's willingness to support or tolerate deviant perspectives. Atheists, who ranked third on this dimension, were close to Communists, who were least tolerated by the American public.

The public also distinguished between allowing the political dissenter a chance to have his say on a "one-shot basis," that is, a speech in the community, and a teaching position at the local high school. Also, 77 percent favored revoking the citizenship of admitted Communists, and 73 percent said they believed it was a good idea for people to report to the Federal Bureau of Investigation any neighbors or acquaintances whom they suspected of being Communists.

We noted in Chapter V that the items on political deviance have not been repeated on subsequent national polls, and we reiterate that it would be useful to do so. The 1950's and 1960's are qualitatively different eras in American life. Much of the 1950's is remembered for its relative political quiescence and social stability. The 1960's was an explosive decade. The blacks, the New Left, the students took to the streets in numbers and intensities not seen in this society since the Civil War era. It would be worthwhile to find out on a comparative and systematic basis how "tolerant" the public is of these expressions of political radicalism and deviance. Does the public, for example, differentiate the New Left from the Communist Party of the 1930's and 1940's? Is it more or less willing to tolerate the entry of the New Left into "sensitive" institutions than it was Communist Party members? Has the over-all level of tolerance been raised or lowered in the decade and a half since the Carnegie survey was conducted? Over the full time span that we have studied the public's responses to issues raised in the national polls, there has been a dearth of items about civil liberties.[12] But particularly during this period of political ferment and activity in

[12]There were some items in the 1960's conceding the right to dissent, with a specific focus on the antiwar demonstrations. Responses to them were reported in Chapter V.

the United States, it would be most useful to collect systematic information that permitted better historical analyses.

In other spheres on the domestic scene, increased disenchantment with the trade-union movement and the power it had achieved in the postwar era was manifested by the fact that in 1952 more than three times as many believed that the laws regulating labor unions were not strict enough compared to those who believed the laws were too strict. By 1959 the ratio had increased to eight to one. In absolute terms, 49 percent said they thought the laws were not strict enough compared to 6 percent who thought the laws were too strict. The other 45 percent were divided almost equally between those who thought the laws were about right and those who had no opinion. On the matter of right-to-work laws, legislation that organized labor directed much of its efforts at defeating, 62 percent of the respondents indicated support.

The public continued its support of traditional welfare capitalism, such as social security and guaranteed minimum hourly wages. On the former, more than two-thirds approved of a proposal to change the law so that persons who received social security would be allowed to earn more than $50 a month. On the latter issue, over 60 percent registered approval for legislation that would raise the minimum hourly wage in 1953 from 75 cents to $1.00, and in 1954 and 1957 from $1.00 to $1.25.

Consistent with a trend that started in the late 1940's, two-thirds also approved of federal aid to public schools as opposed to having the states bear the full burden. Following the Supreme Court's order to many school districts in the South in 1956 and 1957 that they desegregate "with all deliberate speed," the public was asked whether the federal government ought to withhold aid to schools that were still segregated. There was little support for this proposal. In 1956, 32 percent favored withholding aid; a year later the percentage dropped to 17. We remember that in 1956-1957, between 57 and 63 percent said that they approved of the Court's decision. But it is one thing to approve of a law in principle, and another to back that approval with measures that would lead to its effective enforcement. In 1957, the public's mood did not reflect a desire to provide effective regulations that would hasten the widespread implementation of the desegregation decision.

One final comment on the domestic scene in the 1950's. In 1952, just before Dwight Eisenhower and the Republicans took over the reigns of government, the percentage of respondents who believed that the federal income tax they had to pay was too high was 71 percent. This is the highest figure reported in the two and a half decades that the question was asked. By 1959, after a half-dozen years of Republican administration, the percentage dropped to 51, which was about average for peacetime. In 1953, two-thirds of the respondents also said that they thought it more important to balance the budget before reducing income taxes. Balancing the budget is a favorite Republican election issue.

In the area of foreign policy, United States–Soviet relations continued to be a major worry, with special emphasis during this period on the Berlin crisis and the likelihood or desirability of top-level talks between the heads of state of the two countries. China was a major focus of interest, although, unfortunately, there is relatively little national poll data available about American–Chinese relations. The likelihood or desirability of international agreement on banning above-ground nuclear tests was a topic for several national polls during the 1950's. That agreement was reached finally in 1963.

Between 1948 and 1961, there were at least seven polls on the public's assessment of American–Soviet relations in which the public was asked whether it was a good idea for the President (Truman, Eisenhower, or Kennedy) to meet with the Soviet premier, who before 1953 was Joseph Stalin and afterwards was Nikita Khrushchev. Except for two periods, the first in 1948, when the cold war was in its icicle stage and the participants would have been Truman and Stalin, and the second in April 1958, which was immediately after the U-2 incident in which the Soviets shot down an American spy plane flying over its territory, the levels of response indicating support for such a meeting varied only slightly. From February 1950 to January 1961, between 58 and 71 percent said they thought it would be a good idea for the President to meet with the Russian premier to work out more effective plans for peace.

In these data, the public reflected both a sense of optimism that differences could be worked out and a belief that when two men (even if they are heads of major powers) faced each other across a table, complicated issues began to appear resolvable. Americans seemed to feel this most strongly whenever a new President took over the reigns of government. In January 1953, when Eisenhower became President, 69 percent said they thought it would be a good idea for him to meet with Stalin; and in January 1961, 71 percent thought it a good idea for Kennedy and Khrushchev to meet face to face.[13]

The public's adamancy on the issue of retaining troops in Berlin has already been noted. Perhaps there is a relationship between the fact that almost 80 percent consistently favored a strong stand on Berlin and the fact that American expectations about the likelihood of living peacefully with the Soviet Union increased from 23 percent to 46 percent between November 1954 and January 1960. We noted in Chapter VI that in 1938, 54 percent of the American public said they did not expect to have to fight Germany. The percentages reported about the Soviet Union do not indicate such sidespread belief that a war could be avoided. But the responses are worth comparing more because of what they tell us about increased American awareness of the complexities of international involvements and the responsibilities of major powers than because they provide a realistic assessment of the relative dangers to peace that the Soviet Union poses as compared to the threat posed by Nazi Germany two decades earlier.

Between September 1950 and September 1958, on at least seven national polls the public was asked whether it thought the Communist government of China should be permitted to have the Security Council seat at the United Nations in place of the Nationalist government. The percentage supporting such a position ranged from 8 to 20. In absolute terms, these figures are negligible. But they do indicate a slight trend in the direction of a more favorable attitude toward the seating of the Chinese Communists. Unfortunately, few other inquiries about China appeared on national polls during this period.

On the issue of a nuclear test-ban treaty, the American position during the 1950's can be summarized briefly as follows: We will not stop testing atomic or hydrogen bombs until all other nations, including the Soviet Union, agree to do so; 63 percent held such a view. Moreover, 70 percent also favored supporting an international system of inspection to insure that no nation was producing nuclear weapons.

[13] There were no national polls following Kennedy's death and Johnson's inauguration in which this item was asked.

THE KENNEDY–JOHNSON–NIXON YEARS: 1960–1970

In the period beginning in the late 1930's, anti-Semitism was an important "scientific" and political issue. In the same vein, the late 1940's and early 1950's emphasized civil liberties. The decade of the 1960's focused on blacks and their civil rights.

Chapter III reviewed the attitudes of whites and blacks to the civil-rights protests, riots, and demonstrations of the 1960's.[14] In response to an item that asked whether demonstrations by Negroes did more to help or hurt the advancement of civil rights, most whites answered that they thought the demonstrations hurt the Negroes' cause. Most Negroes thought they helped. When given the opportunity to react to specific actions taken by Negroes, such as sit-ins, picketing of political conventions, and boycotts, most whites also disapproved of them.

For years, white leadership in the South argued that all instances of "social unrest" that occurred in their communities was instigated by "outside agitators," usually from the North. In 1965, 78 percent of respondents residing in all parts of the country said they thought Communists to some extent or to a great extent had been involved in the civil-rights demonstrations. Along the same lines, most whites cited outside agitation and Negro laziness and ignorance as the main reasons for the riots. Negroes, in response to the same item, cited prejudice, broken promises, poverty, and lack of jobs as the main reasons. Of the Negro respondents, 91 percent, compared to 34 percent of the whites, said they believed that the race revolt was supported by the rank and file of Negroes.

Chapter III ended on a pessimistic note. The pessimism arose not so much because of white attitudes toward specific issues or activities, but because of the white community's definition of the situation. Even though 76 percent said they were more worried about

[14]The first half of Chapter III reviewed opinion on such matters as the desegregation of public schools, transportation facilities, and neighborhoods; the native intelligence of Negroes; and the advisability of extensive federal intervention into practices that previously had been left to the states. On each of these issues, opinion changed in the direction of greater integration and willingness to accept the Negro as a first-class citizen in the formal institutional spheres of the society. In more intimate spheres, such as entertaining Negroes in one's home or mixed marriages, public acceptance was not high.

race riots in 1967 than they had been a year earlier (in 1966, 49 percent had answered "more worried"), when asked who they thought was more to blame for the conditions in which Negroes found themselves—white people or Negroes—more than two and a half times as many respondents said Negroes were to blame. In 1968, 70 percent said they believed that Negroes in this country were treated the same as whites. Most whites also rejected the conclusion of the President's Commission on Civil Disorders (1968) that our nation was moving toward two societies, "one black, one white . . . separate and unequal." With this frame of reference, it is on the one hand understandable why most white Americans do not believe that the Negroes' demands are legitimate, and on the other hand difficult to predict a peaceful and quick resolution of the problem that would be acceptable to both communities.

Toward the end of the 1960's, partly as a result of Negro demands for their civil rights and the growing sensitivity in American society about "ethnic claims" (American Indians also began to organize and make collective demands), partly as a result of the much-discussed phenomenon of black anti-Semitism, and partly because a long time had elapsed since a careful, comprehensive study of anti-Semitism in the United States had been made, two major works on this topic appeared.[15] In Chapter IV, we discussed the differences in tone between the Stember (1966) study and the Selznick-Steinberg (1969) volume. The former was optimistic; Stember and his associates claimed that much had been well with American Jews during the preceding decade and that the situation would probably continue as it had or would improve. The Selznick-Steinberg view was that conditions had been good but that there were signs which should not be ignored (nor should they be over-dramatized) that perhaps the future would not bode as well for American Jewry. Selznick and Steinberg described a "hard core" of anti-Semitism in the United States and concluded that "if the population as a whole were as anti-Semitic as the most anti-Semitic third, most Americans would be very anti-Semitic indeed."

The evidence from which Stember drew his more optimistic conclusions is the longitudinal data from the national polls. When he compared, as we have done, the responses in the 1960's with

[15] Marx's (1967) study of black anti-Semitism was cited in Chapter IV, and the conclusion that blacks are no more anti-Semitic than whites noted.

those in the 1930's, 1940's, and 1950's, he found a consistent trend in the direction of less anti-Semitism. For example, in the 1930's and 1940's, between 41 and 56 percent said they thought Jews had too much power in the United States. In the 1960's, between 17 and 19 percent said Jews had too much power. In response to items about Jewish quotas at universities, the desirability of Jewish neighbors, the honesty of Jewish businessmen, the desirability of hiring Jewish employees, the drop in anti-Semitic responses was sharp and significant.

Chapter IV ended on a note of restraint and foreboding. We suggested that events in Vietnam and the Middle East, the state of the economy, and the position of the New Left could reverse the trends of the preceding few years and an upsurge in anti-Semitism might result. We do not see this upsurge as a likely event, but neither do we rule it out completely.

The decade of the 1960's witnessed greater support than in previous decades for the extension of existing welfare programs and the introduction of new ones. The Truman administration, for example, had been unable to gain passage of a federally sponsored medical-insurance program. The Eisenhower administration had not advocated such a program. In 1965 President Johnson announced the passage of Medicare, a program that did not differ significantly from the Truman proposal of the late 1940's. That the passage of the Johnson-sponsored Medicare program was consistent with popular sentiment is shown by the fact that there was almost a 100 percent increase in public support of government-sponsored health programs between 1949 and 1965.

In the 1960's, national polls for the first time asked the public for its opinion of a new type of subsidy program whereby the federal government would provide needy families with a minimum annual income. This proposed guaranteed direct financial subsidy would replace the relief and welfare payments that families receive if they meet certain qualifications, such as the absence of a father in the home or a disabled or unemployed father. When the public was asked whether it approved or disapproved of such a program, almost twice as many said they disapproved as supported it. At the same time (1968–1969), the public indicated strong support (78 percent) for a federally sponsored program whereby each family that has an employable wage earner would be guaranteed enough work to give him a wage of about $60 a week or $3,200 a year. The American public, unlike many European societies, was not yet willing to legitimize receiving financial subsidy on a regular, "no questions asked" basis. It did, however, support subsidized work programs whereby the recipients of those subsidies could be shown to have "earned" their incomes. The latter proposal has been presented to the Congress by President Nixon, but has not yet been acted upon.

The public's negative attitude toward a guaranteed annual income and its attitude toward labor unions perhaps go hand in hand. The 1960's witnessed a continuation of the irritation that one sensed in the public's responses to items about trade unionism in the 1950's. In principle, between 66 and 71 percent said they favored labor unions. But a majority also favored right-to-work laws and compulsory arbitration and opposed union shops and featherbedding—all measures that organized labor has perceived as significant threats to its bargaining position with employers.

One of the major reasons for the public's disenchantment with the trade-union movement is the affluence or power that is now associated in the public's mind with that movement. Organized labor has become another major force with which the society must reckon. It is no longer a "have-not," relatively voiceless group fighting for recognition. George Meany, president of the largest combination of trade unions, is an important figure in the establishment. His opinion counts not only on labor-related issues, but on foreign policy as well. In addition, the corruption in some labor unions and the undemocratic internal functioning of others have also had their effect on reducing popular support. Among most of the blacks and the New Left, the trade-union movement is not a potential ally but a powerful force working on the side of the establishment. It is part of the industrial-military complex that they see controlling and subverting the whole society.

A major issue of the 1960's that, as far as public awareness was concerned, was born in that decade was overpopulation. During the depression, as discussed in Chapter II, the concern was with underpopulation, and experts were seeking ways in which to promote larger families. Today with few exceptions—most of them economists such as Colin Clark, Ansley Coale, and Simon Kuznets—many biologists, politicians, and the popular media describe the disastrous consequences to the world and to American society as well if population growth continues at its present rate. As of 1965, only 29 percent of the public said they were worried about population increase. Four years later, in 1969, when asked whether they thought it would be necessary at some time to limit population if present living standards were to be maintained, as many thought it would be necessary as thought it would not be. These responses suggest that the public was not in a panic about overpopulation. The messages delivered so dramatically by Paul Ehrlich in *The Population Bomb* (1968) and by such organizations as Zero Population Growth have not, at least as yet, aroused the American public to a state of panic. This is not to say that they may not have had significant effects on behavior, as witness the report issued in 1971 and cited in Chapter II, which said that the number of preschool children in the United States had declined sharply in the 1960's, so that zero population growth within this century was a distinct possibility.

On two related matters, conditions under which abortions should be performed legally and sterilization programs, most respondents were not in favor of legalizing abortions for financial reasons. The health of the mother and, to a lesser degree, the likelihood of a deformed child were accepted by at least 54 percent of the public as bases for abortion. We reported also that the public, along with some state legislatures, was shifting its position toward a loosening of requirements for abortion. In 1969, 40 percent of the respondents said they favored a law that would permit a woman to go to a doctor to end a pregnancy at any time during the first three months. A few months later, New York state passed such a law, and other states were considering comparable actions. On the question of who should be sterilized, 64 percent said they approved of voluntary sterilization of women who had more children than they could provide for properly. Over 75 percent approved of sterilization if the mother's health was endangered or if persons had mental or physical afflictions and asked to be sterilized. We commented earlier that sterilization on a voluntary basis for an economic reason seemed to be more widely accepted than abortion for the same reason.

One additional comment should be made about interpreting the responses of the public to the abortion and sterilization items. It would be a mistake to interpret the level of support for legalizing abortions or sterilization solely as an index of the level of concern that the public has for the population problem, because one could favor liberalizing and legalizing abortions on grounds of civil liberties and extending individual freedom and choice without regard for overpopulation. Similarly, one could be extremely concerned about overpopulation and not endorse legalizing abortions and/or sterilization programs, but instead advocate other means of population control.

On matters of foreign policy, in the decade of the 1960's more than the previous one, there was one issue that stood out above all others—the war in Vietnam. At the time of writing, the fighting continues, the peace talks in Paris seem hopelessly stalled, and feelings about the rightness and wrongness of the United States position in Vietnam arouse more and more internal conflict. In Chapter VI, we compared attitudes toward the war in Vietnam with the public's position on the Korean conflict and found that there was a similar pattern.

At the outset of both wars, more than twice as many supported as opposed American intervention. Two years later (the war in Korea did not continue much longer than that), public opinion shifted such that more people opposed rather than favored American policy. It took a little longer for the shift to occur on the Vietnam issue, but that is probably because American intervention started out on a more limited basis. It was not as apparent to what extent the United States would intervene in Vietnam in August 1965 or even 1966, whereas in Korea the decision to intervene and the subsequent action followed more closely. But even in the summer of 1965, when 61 percent said they favored our policy in Vietnam, 70 percent also thought that the situation in Vietnam was getting worse rather than better. In 1970, the proportion who said they approved of the way President Nixon was handling the situation in Vietnam ranged from a high of 65 percent in January to a low of 46 in April, shortly before the invasion of Cambodia.

By their responses to questions about the bombings of North Vietnam and their reactions to President Johnson's decision to stop the bombings, most of the public indicated that it supported the adminstration's policies as of April 1968.

The public never indicated much faith in the ability of the South Vietnamese "to go it alone" or to establish a stable government. As of March 1968, the public was divided almost evenly between those who thought the South Vietnamese wanted the United States to remain and those who did not. As of May 1968, 77 percent thought that the war would end with some sort of compromise settlement having been worked out. Only 10 percent expected a clear-cut victory; 4 percent foresaw defeat. A year later, in June 1969, 53 percent said they approved of a suggestion whereby the United States would call for a cease-fire, with both sides staying where they were at that time. Such a stance would have left the North Vietnamese in a better position than would an earlier settlement. In February 1971, 66 percent advocated withdrawal of all American troops by the end of the year.

Not unrelated to the Vietnam issue was the public's perception of China during this period. On this point we refer again to the shift in opinion that occurred in response to the item about which country the public thought would be the greater threat to world peace, Russia or China. In 1961, 49 percent answered Russia, and 32 percent China. In 1967, 69 percent answered China, and 20 percent Russia. At the same time, 46 percent said they believed that if war ever broke out between the United States and China, the Soviet Union was more likely to be on the side of the United States than on the side of China (36 percent thought Russia would ally herself with China). But in 1970, the invitation by the Peking government to the American Ping-Pong team and the announcement by President Nixon shortly thereafter that he would visit China in the next few months influenced public attitudes in the direction of greater willingness to have China represented in the United Nations.

Events in the Middle East since 1967 that have involved the United States as well as the Soviet Union and the recent signs of a thaw in United States-Sino relations may have again altered the public's view as to which country poses the greater threat to world peace and the alignments that are likely to occur should there be a major conflict. From the perspective of the 1960's, it appears that in the decade of the 1970's the situation in the Middle East, relations between the United States and China, and the Vietnam War are likely to be the major foreign-policy preoccupations of the American government.

CONCLUDING REMARKS

By way of conclusion we reiterate a theme that persists throughout the volume, namely, that the American public is more informed about, more involved in, and more committed to the formulation and implementation of national policy than professional observers have described it as being. On domestic issues, particularly those of a bread and butter variety, the public is not only reasonably well informed and prepared to express an opinion, but has on many occasions led or prompted the Congress or the President toward passage of a program that might otherwise have been delayed for months or years. Welfare legislation concerning minimum wages, social security, medical programs, are examples of issues on which public opinion has preceded and prompted government action.

Civil liberties and civil rights, on the other hand, are issues about which public opinion has either lagged behind government policy or tended to support measures that are repressive of constitutional rights. Since the mid-1950's the Supreme Court and, to a lesser extent, the Executive branch of the government have led both the Congress and the public in interpreting and formulating policies and perspectives on civil rights that were more progressive than those shared by the latter groups. In the area of civil liberties, the Congress and the President have quite consistently been able to depend upon the public to support actions and legislation that would contain dissent, that would limit the activities of dissident political groups and that would control expressions of opposition and disagreement with official policy. The public's opposition to deviant political groups and its support of policies that reward conformity were manifest in the 1930's against both the "right" and the "left" and in the 1950's and 1960's most especially against the "left".

The traditional view that the American public is largely ignorant of and indifferent to foreign policy has not been substantiated by this review of the national polls. However true such a characterization may have been in the era following the First World War, it does not apply today and has not applied since the end of the Second World War. The American Public experienced a profound lesson about the dangers of isolationism and the relative advantages of participation in international politics. Its commitment to American participation in and support for the United Nations, its backing of foreign aid programs, nuclear test-ban treaties, are illustrations of the public's change of mind and role.

Political scientists and other professional observers may still be correct in their belief that domestic policy, particularly issues that affect pocketbooks, safety, health, are more salient, and more interesting, to the American public. But the image of an ignorant, indifferent public who neither knows nor cares about the commitments that its government is making, or the image that it is projecting to the rest of the world, is also without empirical basis.

REFERENCES CITED

Acheson, Dean.
   1970. *Present at the Creation.* New York.
Almond, Gabriel.
   1950. *The American People and Foreign Policy.* New York.
Bernstein, B. J., and A. J. Matusow.
   1966. *The Truman Administration.* New York.
Bettelheim, Bruno, and Morris Janowitz.
   1964. *Social Change and Prejudice.* Glencoe, Ill.
Bogue, Donald.
   1961. *Principles of Demography.* New York.
Bryce, James.
   1962. "Modern Democracies." In D. Katz *et al., Public Opinion and Propaganda.* New York.
Clark, Colin.
   1967. *Population Growth and Land Use.* New York.
Coale, Ansley J.
   1968. "Should the United States Start a Campaign for Fewer Births?" *Population Index,* 34 (October-December), 467-474.
Dickinson, John.
   1930. "Democratic Realities and Democratic Dogma." *American Political Science Review,* 24, 283-309.
Douglas, Paul
   1936. *Social Security in the United States.* New York.
Ehrlich, Paul.
   1968. *The Population Bomb.* New York.
Glenn, Norval.
   1970. "Problems of Comparability in Trend Studies with Opinion Poll Data." *Public Opinion Quarterly,* 34, No. 1, 82-91.
Hyman, Herbert H., and Paul B. Sheatsley.
   1956. "Attitudes toward Desegregation." *Scientific American,* 195 (December), 35-39.
Jensen, Arthur R.
   1969. "How Much Can We Boost IQ and Scholastic Achievement?" *Harvard Educational Review,* 39, No. 1, 1-123.
   Newsweek, March 31, 1969, and June 2, 1969.

Kalven, Harry, Jr.
  1965. *The Negro and the First Amendment*. Columbus.
Key, V. O.
  1961. *Public Opinion and American Democracy*. New York.
Kuznets, Simon.
  1960. "Population Change and Aggregate Output." In *Demographic and Economic Change in Developed Countries.* Princeton.
Landsberg, Hans H., *et al.*
  1964. *Natural Resources for U.S. Growth*. Baltimore.
Lipset, Seymour Martin.
  March 1971. *Anti-Semitism in the United States*. A talk in Jerusalem.
Marx, Gary.
  1967. *Protest and Prejudice*. New York.
Myrdal, Gunnar, *et al.*
  1944. *An American Dilemma*. New York.
President's Committee on Civil Rights.
  1947, reprinted 1967. *To secure These Rights*. Washington, D.C.
Public Opinion Quarterly, 34 (Fall 1970), No. 3.
Rainwater, Lee.
  1960. *And the Poor Get Children*. Chicago.
Schwartz, Mildred A.
  1966. *Trends in White Attitudes toward Negroes*. Chicago.
Selznick, Gertrude J., and Stephen Steinberg.
  1969. *The Tenacity of Prejudice: Anti-Semitism in Contemporary America*. New York.
Sheatsley, Paul B.
  1966. "White Attitudes toward the Negro." *Daedalus*, 95 (Winter), 217–237.
Stember, Charles H., *et al.*
  1966. *Jews in the Mind of America*. New York.
Stouffer, Samuel.
  1957. *Communism, Conformity, and Civil Liberties*. New York.
Sykes, Christopher.
  1965. *Cross Roads to Israel*. London.
Truman, David B.
  1951. *The Government Process*. New York.

Verba, Sydney.
   1970. "The Silent Majority: Myth and Reality." *University of Chicago Magazine*, 63, No. 2, 10–19.
Waskow, Arthur I.
   1966. *From Race Riot to Sit In.* New York.

INDEX

(